3-12-79

CHANGING PLACES

Men on women in "men's" jobs:

What work would she be doing? Was she good looking?

We were worried—can we swear? Why would she want a job where she's the only woman?

We didn't think it was right to get a big jump into this job. She shouldn't be taking a man's job.

Was she capable? Would she pull her share of the load?

Some thought they [women] could handle it. Some were bitter. There were jokes about them. Some guys would tell them, Go home to the kitchen—and they meant it. Others were friendly.

Women on men in "women's" jobs:

We didn't think a man could hack it, wouldn't have the patience or tolerance, couldn't do filing, wouldn't be as involved as a woman. He couldn't do *our* job.

We were worried that we'd have to watch our language like about general girl things and personal things, like about your period. We worried about whether we could be ourselves.

The single girls were dying to see what they [the new males] looked like.

We wondered why he was taking *this* job. When we saw him, we said, He's not bad. Then we *really* wondered why he was coming to this job.

We kidded about his having to wear a skirt.

We wondered, What does he look like? Is he strange? Does he wear earrings? No one actually asked if he was straight or gay, since it was some time ago and you didn't talk about things like that. But I think that was behind the jokes about the earrings.

What are the problems a woman
faces when she moves into an occupation traditionally reserved for
males? When men cross job/sex
lines, do they encounter hostility or
welcome?

In *Changing Places*, Carol
Schreiber addresses these and other
questions of immediate concern to
company supervisors and managers,
government attorneys, and others
involved in policymaking and implementation of affirmative action
programs. Students of social organizations and social problems, as well
as the interested reader, will gain
from *Changing Places* a better understanding of the problems encoun-
tered when new job opportunities are
"opened up" for men and women.

Working with the cooperation of a
large company actively promoting
sex-atypical employment among its
personnel, Schreiber interviewed
employees in study and control
groups who made the change to sex-
atypical jobs and those who held jobs
traditionally associated with their sex.
The book balances Schreiber's careful
analysis of interview findings with the
reactions of employees in both
groups who discuss their motivations
for making job changes, their concern
about "making it" and being accepted
on the job, their feelings about one's
place in the job and in the company,
and the attitudes of their co-workers.

CHANGING PLACES

Men and Women in Transitional Occupations

Carol Tropp Schreiber

The MIT Press
Cambridge, Massachusetts,
and London, England

This book was set in VIP Univers
by Grafacon, Inc., and printed
and bound by Halliday Lithograph Corporation
in the United States of America
Library of Congress Cataloging in Publication Data

Schreiber, Carol Tropp.
Changing places.

Based on the author's thesis, Yale.
Bibliography: p.
Includes index.
1. Sex discrimination in employment—United States.
2. Occupational mobility—United States. 3. United
States—Occupations. 4. Job descriptions. I. Title.
HD4903.5.U58S33   331.1'27   79-4279
ISBN 0-262-19177-6

To the memories and inspirations
of my first mentor
E. Richard Weinerman, M.D.,
and my sister Miriam Lee Tropp

CONTENTS

ACKNOWLEDGMENTS

From its beginnings as a dissertation through its transformation into a book, this work has had many collaborators. Some of the most important contributions came from people who cannot be named, since they were in the organization that graciously lent itself as a research site. By naming them, even in gratitude, I would violate a promise of confidentiality. Still, to those in the organization whose teamwork smoothed study development and arrangements, as well as to those who participated as respondents, I express that gratitude and hope that my feedback to them justifies their efforts.

A second major source of support came from faculty members at Yale who contributed to the original study, to the dissertation as it emerged, and in the end to this book. Among those who gave to the original study, Clay Alderfer, my thesis chairman, helped by consistently prodding me to stay on my own track, despite my frequent resistance. He has pushed me into taking more risks than I thought I could. Other faculty members contributed uniquely to the work and to my development. Bob Miles was supportive and appropriately demanding about methodological issues. Jim Rosenbaum was a reflective and insightful colleague with many ideas about how to develop my work and with support when I needed it. John Bassler contributed immeasurably to my understanding of the data and techniques of data analysis and to my ability to integrate quantitative and qualitative materials. Other contributions and ideas were offered by Rosabeth Kanter, Gerrit Wolf, and John Van Maanen. John also made many valuable suggestions for the final manuscript. From the start I have appreciated the quality of his judgment and his generosity. Stan Kasl and Ed Pauly were helpful with reference materials. Garry Brewer, Doug Yates, and Vic Vroom each offered encouragement and guidance in the process of transforming an academic dissertation into a publishable book. Finally, I am grateful to Dan Levinson for his faith and encouragement.

I am thankful to other colleagues for their attention and suggestions about the dissertation and for their moral support. Marie Avitable, Kim Cameron, Faye Crosby, Tom Dulz, Bill Kraus, Rick Guzzo, Irene Loukedes, Nancy McGuerty, Jone Pearce, and Michael Raskin have been very helpful. For specific research assistance for the original project, I thank Robin Golden, Mark Schoenberg, Rich Israel, Dave Bruce, and Gary Mulligan.

First in the production of the dissertation and later in bringing out the book, Jessica Davidson has been a loyal and competent typist whose judgments I have appreciated and valued. Kathy Faught has been cheerfully helpful in reproduction for both efforts.

For their faith I thank the Woodrow Wilson Foundation and the U.S. Department of Labor for dissertation research support. A prize from the Woodrow Wilson Foundation helped with some of the extras involved with the study. Without the support of the Department of Labor, the project would not have been possible. The initial report was prepared for the Employment and Training Administration, U.S. Department of Labor, under Research and Development Grant #91-09-76-44. Grantees conducting research and development grants under government sponsorship are encouraged to express their own judgment freely, and I am solely responsible for the contents of the initial report and the book.

Finally, in the past two years my involvement in the study, the dissertation, and this book have made great demands on the love and patience of my friends and family. My parents, Bernice and Jack Tropp, have been caring and interested. My husband, Sandy Schreiber, has given much of himself and has managed some difficult transitions with grace. Rebecca and Madeline Schreiber, our daughters, have been compassionate and helpful, far beyond their years. I am delighted by their flexibility and enthusiasm. When Rebecca decided that she wanted to become a surgeon and Madeline requested a typewriter for her

ninth birthday, I knew that both the process and content of book preparation had been absorbed by my
family, for better or for worse. I hope that it is for
better and that we have all learned something from
changing places.

Carol Tropp Schreiber

PROLOGUE

When I began this work, I intended to explore one changing feature of the contemporary workplace, that involved with the movement of men and women into work situations previously occupied predominantly by members of the other sex. As I prepared the groundwork for that exploration, I gradually uncovered traces of another kind of change associated with the erosion of jobs and opportunities through the introduction of technological innovation. As I developed the study, I became aware that these two kinds of changes were having separate and contingent effects on the people and places I had selected for my original exploration. Once alerted to the multiple pressures for change in the workplace, I realized that understanding this work situation would not be possible through focus on one kind of change and its effect. Instead I needed to use different lenses to bring into focus the different features of a changing picture of a changing organization.

Here then is an effort to portray my insights into a dynamic and complex work situation, by first presenting *what* I learned through systematic inquiry about the movement of men and women into new work situations. *How* I learned what I learned is a side of the story not readily apparent in this report of findings and thus deserving of special attention. That side of the story encompasses the personal meaning of the study, the development of the systematic inquiry—explication of the research "saga." The research saga details the process of discovery, a history that in itself illuminated and shaped the final product. Although process and product are intertwined and interdependent, each can be highlighted to illuminate its full contours. Each facet offers a contribution to the thought and method of behavioral science.

To highlight both sides of the picture, then, I have chosen to present a full version of the research saga in an epilogue, intended to be read as an integral part of this document. Through this approach, I hope to demonstrate the worth of documenting both conduct and consequences of inquiry. As one report of a generalizable approach to the conduct of inquiry, it marks an attempt to match technology to the task of behavioral science research.

CHANGING
PLACES

1 CHANGING TIMES

Changing Names: His Job/Her Job

In late 1977 the U.S. Department of Labor released the fourth revision of its *Dictionary of Occupational Titles,* a systematic compilation of job definitions, descriptions, and duties. Among the achievements of the fourth revision were its reduction in size from two volumes to one, the deletion of numerous outdated job titles, the addition of other more contemporary positions, and *the elimination of all reference to sex or age in job titles and descriptions.* The impact of this change is illustrated in the following list of job titles and their changes between the 1965 and 1977 versions of the dictionary.

1965 Title	1977 Title
Clergymen	Clergy
Newsboys	Newspaper carriers and vendors
Stock and bond salesmen	Stock and bond sales agents
Cranemen, derrickmen, and hoistmen	Crane, derrick, and hoist operators
Boatmen and canalmen	Boat operators
Railroad brakemen	Railroad brake operators and couplers
Cleaners and charwomen	Building interior cleaners
Airline stewardesses	Flight attendants
Guards and watchmen	Guards
Maids and servants, private household	Private household cleaners and servants.[1]

In his preface to the fourth revised version of the DOT, Ernest Green, assistant secretary of labor for employment and training, remarked that the current volume could be used as a resource for increased information about work and employment, and in turn, as a piece of social policy intended to help in achieving "the objective of restoring a high employment economy with productive employment opportunities for all groups."[2] He continued:

Our labor force has grown by almost one third in this relatively short period, from less than 75 million to over 97 million. Women now make up over 40 percent of all workers, as compared with about 35 percent a dozen years ago, and a continuously increasing proportion of both men and women workers are employed in service producing rather than goods producing industries. Reflecting the high birth rates following World War II, record numbers of young Americans graduated from the Nation's high schools and colleges and began looking for work. Unfortunately, we have not been able to generate new job opportunities rapidly enough in recent years to provide productive avenues of employment for all such workers or for many women and minority workers seeking full participation in the American economy.[3]

Green's hopes were echoed by the introductory words of Ray Marshall, secretary of labor in 1977. From the Department of Labor perspective, various kinds of change were intended in this revised lexicon of occupational terminology. Of central import was the implied challenge to colloquialisms and conventions that sustained job definitions, descriptions, and duties: their very names specified the kind (sex) of person who was right for the job.

The changes in the *Dictionary of Occupational Titles* are but one facet of a large-scale government effort to extend equal opportunity to the workplace. Within the past decade the federal government has extended its concern and activity about individual civil rights into work organizations. This concern was mandated through a series of legislative, judicial, and executive actions that together affect most work organizations directly or indirectly.[4] Through direct compliance mechanisms organizations have been required to make restitution for past employment inequities and to redistribute work opportunity and payment equitably among present and future employees.[5] In spirit this mandate intends to equalize employment and promotion opportunity for women and members of specific minority groups—the "protected" classes. In letter the manadate requires institutions to reexamine their policies regarding selection and placement of female and minority employees and to develop detailed plans to correct imbalance. On the basis of these plans for corrective (affirmative) action, many work organizations have been required to revise selection and placement procedures for female and male workers.

Governmental effort to change policy and practice in regard to the distribution of work opportunity and the sex-stereotyping of jobs has taken many forms, one of which is represented by the DOT. No matter what its form, or for that matter its rate of progress, neither governmental activity nor organizational response has occurred in a social vacuum. During the 1960s and 1970s changes in governmental regulation and organizational policy have coincided with relevant demographic social and economic trends, trends that have particularly affected the participation of women in the work force. The number of employed women has doubled between 1950 and 1974, to a point where women now constitute 40 percent of all workers.

The increasing number of women in the work force combined with governmental activity and pressure has meant moves for some women into work situations previously occupied predominantly or solely by men. Still, the largest numbers of female workers have remained in clerical work, where their proportions of the total have increased from 69 percent to 78 percent between 1962 and 1974, and in other bastions of female employment such as hairdressing, food counterwork, sales clerking, and nursing. Despite the stability of overall patterns of occupational distribution, there have been some changes in the composition of jobs not traditionally occupied by females. Between 1962 and 1974, for example, there were dramatic increases in the proportion of female busdrivers (12 to 37percent), bartenders (12 to 33 percent), and bakers (18 to 41 percent). At the same time, there were smaller but still visible increases in the proportions of male telephone operators (3.7 to 6.2 percent), librarians (14.3 to 18.3 percent), and registered nurses (1.5 to 2 percent).[6] Recent statistics, then, present a mixed picture of trends in occupational sex composition. While some figures hint at changes in job occupancy for men and women, others document more stable patterns of male and female distribution in most jobs and occupations.

Front Page News

Although statistics portray some gradual change in the overall composition of certain jobs, another source of contemporary information—the mass media—has presented a different kind of picture. Headlines and feature stories, situation comedies, and TV commercials have broadcast a different image of occupational and social change—an image that appears to be "larger than life." Individuals and their unique moves into nontraditional positions have been spotlighted in a variety of ways by the different media. One television series, "All that Glitters," created situation comedy from the interactions of men and women in nontraditional work and family positions. Another source of information, a weekend edition of the local newspaper, contained seven highly visible features about men and women in sex-atypical occupations, from a story headlined "This Is Your Pilot Speaking, She Said"[7] to a comedienne's quip "I think it's great that we're having sexual equality in all areas. I was just discussing that very point with my Avon man this morning."[8] The topic of occupational change by both sexes could not be avoided and was in fact visibly dramatized.

Media coverage of occupational change for men and women has highlighted two facets of the phenomenon: a more serious side, which reports the legal battles of those prevented from making occupational changes, and the "cuter" approach, which focuses on the unique individual who has succeeded in an unusual occupation. Stories about these unique representatives have emphasized "human interest" and the special quality of their work experience, often with an emphasis on the protagonist's heroism or humorous response to an unusual work situation. Rarely have our journalists raised the kinds of question that might nick the heroic facade. Attention to glamour and drama has ignored some of the questions that might be asked of those who have made moves and changes in such stable aspects of our social structure and has prevented us from learning much about what has actually happened.

Behind the Front Page

As a rare example of her kind, writer Nora Ephron raised some of these questions in an *Esquire* article on Bernice Gera, first female umpire. Ephron was baffled:

I cannot understand any woman's wanting to be the first woman to do anything. I read about those who do—there is one in today's newspaper, who is suing the State of Colorado for the right to work on a team digging a tunnel through the Rocky Mountains—and after I get through puzzling at the strange desires people have, awe sets in. I think of the ridicule and abuse that woman will undergo, of the loneliness she will suffer if she gets the job, of the role she will assume as a freak, of the smarmy and inevitable questions that will be raised about her heterosexuality, the derision and smug satisfaction that will follow if she makes a mistake, or breaks down under the pressure, or quits. It is a devastating burden and I could not take it, could not be a pioneer, a Symbol of Something Greater.[9]

As Ephron wondered about Bernice Gera and sought her out for interview, so may we wonder about others who have moved into positions not previously occupied by others of their sex. What are the "strange desires" that lead to these kinds of occupational moves? Do these people undergo ridicule and abuse once the moves are made? How do they feel about their positions? Is there loneliness once they get the job? Are questions raised about their heterosexuality? What happens when they make a mistake? Does the move bring a "devastating burden"? What happens to those who do "make it"?

Until now neither journalists nor their scholarly counterparts have raised questions about the personal meaning of these work changes to those who have made them. We have asked little and know little about the changes in the workplace that have been brought about by current social, political, and economic trends. We have asked little and know little about the individual expectations and attitudes fostered by large-scale social conditions. While we have attended to the drama of the phenomenon, we have rarely looked behind the scenes and have learned very little about what has actually happened to men and women who have made these changes.

Now that the phenomenon has been called to our attention and work transitions have been made by more than a few individuals, we can undertake systematic inquiry about men and women who have moved into positions traditionally occupied by members of the other sex. Beginning with Ephron's awe and curiosity, we might ask, What are the motives, hopes, and expectations of those who make these work changes? How do they feel about their work? How do they describe their initial and current work experiences? Do their feelings, experience, or behavior differ from the experiences of persons who occupy jobs or positions traditionally occupied by others of the same sex? How are the "new types" of male and female employees viewed by those already in the jobs they enter? What are the expectations, concerns, and attributions made by supervisors and peers? How do supervisors behave toward the "new types"? Is their behavior different from that typically addressed to "same types," those who make moves into jobs already occupied by others of the same sex? Do men and women have different experiences when they move into positions where they are different from others in those positions? If there are differences between those who have made sex-atypical moves and those who have not, how can they be understood? If there are differences in the experiences and expectations between men and women who make the moves into sex-atypical positions, how can these differences be understood?

The Study: Preview

These questions guided the initial development of this study. I was interested in learning more about work transitions and their meaning for the men and women who had undertaken them. The original focus of this study was on the work experience of men and women who had moved into technical, clerical, and craft jobs previously occupied predominantly by members of the other sex. I was particularly interested in understanding more about the immediate responses of men and women who had moved into these jobs within the past five years, and I wanted to compare these responses with those of men and women in jobs occupied predominantly by members of their own sex.

Fortunately, an opportunity for this kind of study became available with a large work organization that had sponsored changes in the membership of traditionally sex-typed departments. The company itself was interested in the individual, group, and organizational implications of these changes for individuals who had made transitions and for their work groups. The organization's questions, combined with my own hypotheses and exploratory questions drawn from behavioral science theory and research, helped shape the study.

Because this organization's problem matched my interest as a researcher, this type of study represents a form of "action research." Action research, as originally proposed by the social psychologist Kurt Lewin in the early 1940s, seeks to combine social usefulness with scientific meaning. To accomplish these combined objectives, this type of work must demonstrate characteristics such as relevance to problems with social implications; relevance of results to a concrete situation; opportunity to use the results in that social situation; systematic inquiry; possibility of replication of approach and results; applicability of findings beyond the specific problem (generalizability).

The demands of action research are rigorous; they require attention to immediate organizational issues as well as to general theoretical, empirical, and methodological concerns of behavioral science. How these demands were met has been one focus of my attention, although I will consider here only the phases of the project that led to the collection and interpretation of the data. I will write a separate report and consideration of the feedback and use of the study by the organization.

Paradoxically my commitment to action research may compete with the detachment necessary to carry out a disciplined research program. Recently prominent behavioral scientists have begun to propose a revised form of objectivity for the social researcher. Such objectivity appreciates the historicism of our discipline, noting its correspondence to variability in contemporary events and attitudes. From this point of view the task of the social researcher is not to discover "true and immutable" laws of human interaction, since immutability is not considered a characteristic of human behavior. Rather our work entails a systematic focus on present (and past) social phenomena, with an eye to nonevaluative descriptions of people and their relationships. Such an approach warns us to view our own concepts and operations with humility, with an appreciation for the vagaries of time and situation. Similarly we are warned to think skeptically and dispassionately about theories and findings, to be aware that the works themselves in their dissemination may influence the very social phenomena we study.[10] Certainly a research report about a contemporary social experiment runs this risk.

The Study: My View

I hope that my personal commitment to the research questions is visible from behind the serious scholarly scrim. To heighten that visibility, I should note that this study has had great importance to me as a person and in my role as a behavioral science researcher. The research problem has engaged me on many levels.

At first I was drawn to it because of my own experiences in two different occupations, one sex-typed as "female" (social work) and one sex-typed as "male" (academic scholarship about organizations). A second source of my engagement comes from the promise of social consequence, which has met a personal need for social relevance in my own work. Clearly my experience and values have had a strong impact on my selection of a subject for study and perhaps as much influence on the manner of investigation, analysis, and report.

Personal engagement made the process of doing and writing about the research lively, turbulent, and rich with struggle. I hope this struggle will emerge from the printed page to engage the reader and stimulate discussion and argument.

2 DIRECTIONS AND QUESTIONS

Beginnings: His Job/Her Job

When Ephron introduced Bernice Gera, she made a common assumption—that the position of baseball umpire was a "man's job." In this culture at this time few of us would question her assumption. Our readiness to share this assumption has been equally apparent in both our colloquial conversations and scholarly works. On the whole, professional observers of society, such as historians, anthropologists, sociologists, psychologists, economists, and political scientists, have agreed that there is intracultural consensus about what constitutes "male" and "female" work. These scholars have agreed less frequently about the causes, sources, and implications of this intracultural consensus. Depending on their discipline, their generation, their political orientation, and recently their feminist propensities, "authorities" have attributed both causation and implication of the sexual division of labor to different features of the human condition. That such differences have occurred among the most careful social observers marks an important starting point for a study about occupational sex-typing.

Antecedents

Sex Differentiation and Occupations

In one of her earlier works, *Male and Female,* Margaret Mead noted that the division of labor and task by sex was a characteristic of every human society known to anthropologists. Somehow, she noted, there was often little association between the task or work requirements and the abilities or characteristics of the sex to which work was assigned. Often the same task or position was assigned to one sex in one culture and to the other sex in another culture. Although arbitrary and unpredictable in content, there was continuity of form—a division of labor assigned by sex.[1]

Few social observers would disagree with Mead's general observations about the presence of a sexual division of labor in every society. But among these observers there is reasoned disagreement about the sources and purposes of such a division of labor. This disagreement seems to transcend disciplinary boundaries and depend more on the generation and political orientation of the scholar.

For instance, until recently many scholars accepted the sexual division of labor as a biological "given," a social form that derived from the basic reproductive differences between male and female. This school of thought generally assumed that because of women's reproductive capacities, their work functions centered on the "breeding and feeding" aspects and activities of social and work life. Understanding the sexual division of labor was fairly simple from this perspective, since tasks and responsibilities could be divided clearly along these dimensions. From this point of view there seems to have been little tendency to see cultural variations in task and in the organization of work, only tendency to see similarities based on the biological given between societies of different levels of complexity.

A second school of thought, pronounced among anthropologists and sociologists, has been exemplified by the anthropologist Levi-Strauss[2] and the sociologist Caplow,[3] who tended to add a functional component to their considerations. Thus the division of labor by sex was viewed as the primary differentiating characteristic of the occupational world within various cultures. From this universal base certain crucial social functions were implemented. Levi-Strauss suggested that the sexual division of labor created an interdependence between males and females that ensured heterosexual marriage and, in turn, the stability and continuity of a culture. Thus social purpose reinforced biological determination of work activity. This perspective enabled scholars to probe more deeply into the differences between cultures to elaborate on the work done by each sex in different societies, but it explained the details of those differences on the basis of their functionality.

Recently a more skeptical perspective has appeared in the scholarly literature. This perspective is not limited to one discipline but is shared by feminists and by more radical scholars. It has recognized the basic contribution of the reproductive function but has moved beyond the appreciation of biological universality to a consideration of the *differences* between societies in the forms taken by men's and women's work.[4] These scholars have looked to differences for understanding hierarchy and dominance, power and wealth, within a particular society. While it does not ignore previous work of scholars in this area, this perspective has emphasized variability in the kinds of work done by men and women and has disagreed with those who have propounded a model based simply on biological determinism. Once we have moved beyond the assumption of biological determinism, we can observe that patterns and methods of childbearing and childrearing have differed from society to society, even with simple agrarian societies, that our current patterns are not "given" and "universal" but rather may reflect or reinforce other social and economic forces for which the biological attribution may serve as a convenient explanation. For these scholars, then, examining the patterns of hierarchy and power is central to understanding the patterns and potentials of *who does what* work within a given social order.

By emphasizing the different forms taken by men's and women's work in different societies, some contemporary scholars have proposed that the patterns of job assignment by sex are not biologically, but rather socially and economically, determined, that biology is not destiny, and that the fact of a division of labor by sex is not sufficient explanation for any particular pattern of occupational distribution by sex.[5]

This perspective may help to interpret characteristics of our own culture, where assignment of work to women and men has demonstrated patterns of stability as well as change over the years. Historians have informed us, for instance, that work deemed appropriate for one sex has changed during historical periods. In our country during times of national emergency marked by high employment (such as war), women have been readily called to do jobs normally reserved for men, such as heavy assembly-line work. This work may have been viewed as inappropriate—perhaps too difficult—during periods of low employment. On the other hand, during times of national emergency marked by low employment (such as depression), general attitudes about women's capability to do men's work have become more restrictive.[6] In this respect both culture and economic trends may influence conceptions of occupations and beliefs about who "belongs" within a particular occupation.

This cyclic and cultural variability has been overshadowed by a more pervasive and stable trend in occupational sex-typing in our culture. For instance, in the United States no matter what proportion of adult women has participated in the work force (and that number has gone from 18 percent in 1890 to 49 percent in 1977, with women representing 16 percent of the work force in 1890 and 41 percent in 1977), the *types* of jobs held by women have not changed. The occupations that were predominantly female in 1900 are predominantly female in 1977. On a corollary note, women's jobs have generally emphasized similar clusters of tasks and characteristics, including "traditional housewives' tasks like cooking, cleaning, sewing, and canning; distinctive welfare or cultural orientation; few or no strenuous physical activities and hazards; patience, waiting, routine (receptionists, sales workers, telephone operators); rapid use of the hands and fingers; contact with young children; and sex appeal."[7]

These characteristics of women's occupations have

in turn constrained occupational choice for women *and* men. Most often occupations characterized as "female" have been limited to women, implying some limitation in choice of these kinds of occupations for men. On the other hand, because women have been limited to participation in occupations characterized as "typically female," they have been limited in the range of other occupational choices available to them. For example, 50 percent of working women in 1970 were distributed in 21 occupations, while 50 percent of working males were distributed in 65 occupations.[8] Thus one concomitant of the differentiation of labor by sex is a differential rate of participation in different types and numbers of jobs.

Sex-Typed Work: Definitions and Implications

While it may not be difficult to describe empirically the characteristic tasks generally associated with "women's work," it is difficult to come up with a more comprehensive and inclusive definition of sex-typed work.

How do we know when an occupation is or has been sex-typed? Must we rely solely on language and labels? Must we address the question individually with an array of occupational titles? Surprisingly, the large literature that attests to occupational sex-typing rarely defines a sex-typed job or occupation. One scholarly definition with commonsense appeal contends that "occupations can be described as sex-typed when a very large majority of those in them are of one sex and when there is an associated normative expectation that this is as it should be."[9]

For more specific operational definitions of the sex-typed occupation, there are limited resources, as well as some differences of opinion, among those who have thought about the problem systematically. Proposals for calling an occupation sex-typed have varied: more than 50 percent occupancy by one sex,[10] more than 70 percent occupancy by one sex,[11] equivalent to the proportion of the labor force that was one sex at the time of study.[12] A most specific operational definition of the sex-typed occupation used current labor force participation rates plus or minus 5 percent. Any occupation that employed 5 percent more than the proportion of females or males in the labor market was identified as sex-typed; any occupation that employed 5 percent less than the proportion of females or males in the labor force was defined as atypical for the less-represented sex.[13] Most of these operational definitions of occupational sex-typing attempt to link occupational proportions with overall work-force proportions, a most logical connection. Despite their specificity, these definitions and formulas leave room for improvement since they do not include consideration of contemporary norms, attitudes, and history.

For these reasons an intuitively appealing and empirically useful definition of sex-typed occupation might combine these emphases. I propose that any formulation should include consideration of proportions, shared norms and expectations, and history. That is, any contemporary definition of a sex-typed occupation must take into account the historical composition and normative expectations attached to that occupation in the appreciation of its sex-typed status.

Definitions, statistics, and theory all suggest that occupational sex-typing and occupational labels combine with social norms to determine the general consensus about who belongs in what occupational group. This consensus contributes to the construction of boundaries around occupations that are clearly typed. These boundaries limit participation within the occupation to members of one sex.

The segregation of job by sex then poses a barrier for both sexes to participation in work identified with the other sex. Thus it might seem that both men and women have been constrained by limits on occupational choice, limits that have bounded individual decision making with culturally shared assumptions about "men's work" and "women's work." But statistics suggest that while barriers to unencumbered choice *do* exist, those barriers have impeded movement more for women than for men. Similarly occupational segregation by sex has been treated more as a "problem" for women than for men.

Behind the general contention that occupational sex-typing affects both sexes are more specific observations about differences for the sexes created by differences in the effects and ramifications of sex-typing within a particular culture. In our culture, for instance, it has generally been observed that men occupy more occupational positions and higher-status positions. Scholars and laypersons alike have generally agreed that in our culture occupations known as "male" have received more social recognition and reward than those labeled "female." It has been proposed that the different valuation placed on men's and women's work is universal and that women's work is generally assigned lower value in most cultures. A recent experiment has demonstrated that when women in our culture move into occupations or institutions occupied predominantly by men, the prestige of those professions and institutions diminishes.[14]

With these observations in mind, it should be clear that when we speak of new individuals moving into positions previously associated with members of the other sex, we are speaking of two facets of a phenomenon. The first derives from the sexual division of labor, differentiation by function, and subsequently by occupation. This differentiation creates boundaries around particular kinds of work that limit entry into that kind of work mostly to one sex. Individuals are assigned to these occupations according to sex, and members of the same culture generally share beliefs about who belongs in that occupation. The second facet of the phenomenon derives from structure, position, and status. This facet also reflects shared norms within a culture, but it pertains to the *value* attached to a particular occupation or type of occupation. Generally, in this culture and in others, occupations and tasks assigned to men acquire and carry more value or prestige than those assigned to women.

These two facets of sex-typing and sex-segregation of jobs become differentially important when we consider the occupancy of men's jobs by women and women's jobs by men.

Crossing Boundaries and Boundaries to Crossing

From this compilation of materials I have derived a picture of occupational sex-typing and segregation supported by evidence about historical patterns. With this general background, the experiences of individual men and women who have made work transitions can be appreciated in context.

As of early 1978 there had not yet been a systematic empirical study of men and women moving into jobs sex-typed as appropriate for the other sex. No empirical literature has considered and compared the experience of men and women, although there have been some recent conceptual considerations such as the work by Kanter, which helped to shape this study.[15] The literature about men and women in sex-atypical jobs has in fact been quite discrete and different. One body of material pertains to women in male positions; much of this work has been produced by female scholars in academic settings. Numerous articles and books have been produced by women academics about women academics and professionals. On the other hand, material about men in women's occupations has most often appeared in journals of specific professions or occupations. As far as I know, no books or monographs have been devoted to the male experience in an occupation typed as female.

Until recently most of the pertinent literature about movement into sex-atypical occupations has dealt with the participation of women in high-status male occupations, such as law, medicine, science, aca-

demics, or corporate management. Most of the
literature about men in women's jobs has been generated within occupations or "semiprofessions" such
as nursing, social work, librarianship, elementary
education, and more recently, child care work, and it
has been disseminated through professional journals.
The flavor of the two literatures, that about women in
male occupations and that about men in the female
domain, is distinctly different in many respects, but it
shares some common features.

Women in Male Occupations

Behavioral scientists who have attended to changes
in sex composition within occupational groups
have been female behavioral scientists frequently studying women entering high-status male
occupations. Topics of interest have included women
in law, academics, management, and the "professions."[16] Little or no attention has been directed to the
study of women in the lower-status skilled or semi-
skilled trades and occupations traditionally occupied
by men.[17]

In one of the few comprehensive scholarly approaches to the movement of women into a high-
status male occupation, Epstein studied the place of
the female lawyer in the late 1960s and discerned
clear patterns of dilemma and difficulty for the female
entrant. She focused on the structural and ideological
issues that sustained women's place outside the legal
occupation and subsequently identified characteristic
personal experiences reported by women who had
entered the occupation. These experiences included
exclusion from the social networks formed by peers
and limitations on the protégé system typically available to young male lawyers. This behavior, she
suggested, was due to the male image of the profession and the reluctance of women to violate this
image by seeking closer contact or involvement with
male professionals.

In addition to the experiences and behaviors that affected their occupational lives, women lawyers experienced certain difficulties in relation to work itself. Within the work setting the woman was handicapped by the self-consciousness of her position as a woman, designated as attention to sex status. This pattern was similar to the position of the stigmatized person whose visibility created an unusual need for impression management. A similar related phenomenon, identified as a need to "prove themselves," was expressed by female lawyers, no matter how long they had occupied their positions. For example, one female lawyer asserted, "If you make a fool of yourself, you're a damn fool woman instead of just a damn fool."[18] According to Epstein, such attitudes, behaviors, and concerns seemed to characterize the experience of striving members in blocked opportunity structures, which implies that these feelings might be shared by men in positions similar to those occupied by female lawyers.

Epstein's study, conducted in the late 1960s and published in 1970, remains the most thorough inquiry into the situation of women in a typically male occupation. Although a number of other studies have been reported, they have been far less comprehensive in the quality of their data sources and in their interpretation of psychological and structural data. Similarly, within the past decade a number of personal documents have been produced that have given testimony to the experience of individual women in typically male occupations such as medicine. None of this anecdotal information has been collected and thoroughly analyzed using sophisticated tools of analysis. Similarly limited is Hennig's study of twenty-five women in corporate management.[19] It offers some insight into the experience of twenty-five unique individuals, but it provides little information about what actually happened to these women in their positions, how they felt about the day-to-day social climate of their organizations, and the meaning of their careers and career development patterns. Hennig's central interest seems to have been the origins (the how and why of these paths to an executive career) rather than the actual experience or its personal meaning for the individuals in the slots.

A less scholarly but more "on target" contribution is Wetherby's recent publication of conversations with women in all "walks of [male] life."[20] This book enhances some of the interpretations offered by Epstein with interview material rarely reported in other studies of women in male jobs. Wetherby spoke with twenty-two women in jobs ranging from butcher to law school dean. Her questions were somewhat sterotypic, as were the interview reports themselves. Yet the volume provides one of the few sources of personal, anecdotal information about the experiences of individuals who moved into positions where there had been few like them in the past.

Of the first woman pilot for a small commercial airline, the interviewer asked: "What's it like to be the first woman pilot?"

When I started, there was so much going on that it was kind of hard at first. The first year everyone was wondering if I was going to stick around. I felt pressured somewhat. But within about a year, the attitude of the other pilots began changing and they started accepting me as one of the fellows. . . .

I think the biggest problem for me to get over was that young women used to grow up being programmed to be a nurse or housewife or secretary. Doing anything else was a little extraordinary. So I had to get psychologically over this myself. I put a lot of pressure on myself and got through it all right, but I had to go through a period of readjustment with myself. . . .

When I got hired, I did feel pressure because I wanted to do a good job, mainly for women.

I wanted to do a good job so I probably put more pressure on myself than the average individual would. If there had been other women in the same capacity, there wouldn't have been as much pressure.[21]

To questions about being the only woman competing among men, a race car driver responded:

A lot of people ask me what it's like to be the only woman Top Fuel driver. Well, you're singled out. Sometimes it isn't easy because people expect so much from you.

Men say women can't do it. That's the easy way, don't give them a chance. That way you keep the gals out of it.

Before I proved myself, the fellows were a little hard on me. I'd hear stuff around the pits. They didn't really think a gal could do it. But right from the start I beat the boys. *From the start!* It took me a while to gain their respect, but now the fellows would do anything in the world for me. . . .

I like a lot of the fellows. I don't date them even though some of them I would like to date. But I don't because of the situation. I can't because drag racers—they're the best people in the world, but they can be cruel. They're hard on the gals. And I can't take that chance.

I would say that it has been a costly and grueling experience. It took a lot out of me. I had to sacrifice a lot.

I was a little bit hard of nose before because I knew I had a fight on my hands. But I got over that. I grew out of that. I was just a hard racer, and I wanted to win. I wanted to be accepted. And I was not the easiest gal in the world to get along with, because I knew what I wanted.[22]

When Men do "Women's Work"

At first glance there are few similarities between the literature about men who enter occupations typically associated with females and that about women who have moved into male positions. Among the obvious differences between the two literatures is the type of occupation studied. The literature about men in women's jobs draws evidence from the experience of males in nursing, social work, child care, librarianship, and elementary school education—all fields commonly referred to as semiprofessions. Within these fields the position and experience of the male workers has received some attention, especially in recent years.

Just as the literature about women in male occupations has changed somewhat with the advent of feminist awareness and scholarship, so has the literature about men in women's jobs changed. In this respect the studies of men in women's occupations seem to be marked by historical differences in tenor

and style. For example, one frequently cited study of
male nurses conducted in the early sixties portrayed the male nurse as preoccupied with prestige and respect and a victim of low self-esteem, unlike his female counterparts in the same hospital.[23] The same study suggested the reasons for this personal condition were that "it is more or less unrespectable to a man, and hence damaging to his prestige and self-esteem, to be a member of the nursing profession, an occupation in which a large majority of the job incumbents are women," that "in our society, the male winner of a competition with women has but a shallow victory," and that "there is less opprobrium and more prestige attached to the woman who is successful in the male occupational sphere than the man who is in the woman's."[24] Nursing was not considered a legitimate mobility step for men. Finally Segal, in his 1962 article, concluded that men would not be considered successful in women's occupations until they had moved into positions of authority over females in these fields.

In the fifties and sixties the literature of social work reflected views similar to those Segal expressed about nursing. Writing in 1958, a prominent social work spokesperson observed that "the prestige of social work is . . . adversely affected because it is identified as a woman's profession."[25] Like others, this author claimed that the movement of men into social work would increase the status of the profession. A vivid portrayal of this philosophy was reflected in the television series about social work "East Side, West Side," broadcast in the early sixties. The star of this series was George C. Scott, who played a social worker with a job in one of New York's neighborhoods characterized by poverty and crime. Then as now the majority of social workers were female, and the image presented in this television series was unusual. It did not reflect the gender or style of the modal worker in the field. On the other hand, Scott embodied the heroism necessary to enliven a TV series and, not inconsequentially, the charisma to attract males to the occupation. Such attraction was important to those in social work who sought to "upgrade" this occupation.

Some writers in social work and nursing, two fields traditionally associated with women, were thinking about the movement of men into the occupations in the early 1950s. The social work literature makes it clear that there was a deliberate effort to counter the stereotypic view of the occupation as "feminine" with the encouragement of more male entrants. Such an effort and awareness is not immediately apparent from the literature on nursing. Still, both sets of writings openly recognized the lack of prestige associated with the female occupation and the difficulty that such a lack of prestige creates for the male professional.

Explicit acknowledgment of the import of prestige has faded from the literature of both occupations during the seventies. Recently there has been less outright talk about prestige and more focus on the personal and situational issues created by stereotypes and expectations for men who move into occupations predominantly occupied by women. In this respect a 1971 paper about male nurses asserted, "Since a male is not expected to be a nurse, he is apt to be self-conscious of his role, and finds his identity as a nurse to be problematical and even precarious."[26]

Another paper about nursing, published in 1973, suggested that although the number of male nursing school graduates rose from 1 percent of all graduates in 1970 to 3 percent in 1973, it was still difficult being a male nurse. Generally, the article contends, one of two kinds of motivation is attributed to the male who chooses nursing as a career, neither positive. The male nurse is considered either "queer" or driven to reach the top of the heap. Still another attribution was reported by one male nurse: "Men always think you're just doing nursing while you go on to become a doctor. They never really accept you for what you are." In the same vein there was general pressure on the male nurses to prove their masculinity, through talk about sexual prowess and sports: "This is the pressure forced on us as a minority group in this profession."[27]

Similarly, in some recent social work literature an author who earlier emphasized the low prestige of social work as a female occupation has taken a different stance. In reporting an empirical survey of men in social work, Kadushin made no reference to prestige but focused on the specific position and "role" of the man in social work. His study generated little support for his hypotheses about "role strain" and consequent discomfort caused for males in social work. Instead he found that the male social workers surveyed were either more comfortable with their positions than the author had anticipated or more uncomfortable about expressing their discomfort in a questionnaire than the study had anticipated.[28]

There seems to have been little change in the emphasis on administrative pathways for men in social work and nursing.[29] Reports in professional social work journals indicate that men occupy proportionately more positions than women as administrators of social service agencies[30] and as deans and teachers in schools of social work.[31] Kadushin *recommends* that male social workers move toward administrative positions, noting that such movement will help to counteract whatever personal discomfort is evoked by the male position in a female profession. In much the same vein men in social work have been encouraged to concentrate their work in the more "masculine" subspecialties of the field such as administration and community organization, most explicitly for earning advantages but perhaps to counteract discomfort as well.

Men and Women: Common Themes and Shared Perspectives

On the face of it there seem to be few similarities between observations of men in women's occupations and women in men's occupations. Differences are far more visible at first. Most of what has been written about women in men's jobs has been about high-status jobs including the high-paid professions such as medicine and law. Recent additions to this body of knowledge include some reports about women in less prestigious pursuits, although the careers dramatized by Wetherby still carry an aura of glamour. Women have had *more* male occupations to move into than men have had female occupations to pursue (according to the numbers of occupations traditionally assigned to women and men). Thus in many respects it is logical to find more movement of women into traditionally male fields and, in turn, more writing about women in traditionally male fields than vice versa. This pattern is consistent; and there are far fewer descriptions and discussions of men in female positions.

I have the impression that most of the activity and the writing about men in female occupations comes from two fields—nursing and social work. Both occupations, although of higher status than many female-typed occupations, are less prestigious than the male-dominated and male-typed occupations with which they share professional responsibility and turf (specifically medicine). Thus both occupations are less prestigious than other occupations in the same work context and are generally known as semiprofessions. This distinction is important because it has been reported as part of the experience of the male who enters the typically female occupations. Contending with the difference in prestige and status attached to a female job is a challenge faced by men in these positions and not by women in male jobs.

Still there are some surprisingly similar and subtle challenges faced by men and women who have taken atypical positions. In addition to the very visible differences between the male and female situations, there are some thematic similarities. First and most obviously, women in men's jobs and men in women's

jobs are similar because they occupy situations different from the "modal worker" in their overall occupational group. In this respect the position of the
female lawyer is comparable to the position of the
male nurse, and in fact the comparability has been
documented in descriptions of experiences that are
similarly highly visible and self-conscious. The articles and books that I have reviewed reveal another
common theme pertaining to attributions about these
men and women. Similar attributions are made about
men in women's jobs and women in men's jobs, although the quality of the attributions differs. Men
have to contend with questions about why they took
the job in the first place and with expectations of
effeminacy or ambition. Women are questioned
about "femininity" and the seriousness of their commitment to the occupation. Most reports describe
some form of initial social exclusion and discomfort.
Such discomforts, questions, and attributions are experienced both internally and interpersonally, and
they create distress for the men and women who have
moved into these new positions.

The most visible similarity between the reported
experiences of men and women in sex-atypical occupations is this report of distress. No matter how this
distress is explained—and it is explained differently in
different eras for the different sexes—distress is present in both situations. What is there about these situations that makes them so distressing?

Movement into a job typically associated with the
other sex represents a change for an individual. Two
types of change can be linked with the experience of
men and women who have moved into sex-atypical
jobs. One pertains to the process of *movement* into
the sex-atypical position; the other pertains to the
occupancy of a sex-atypical position. The first change,
which is a transition, has been noted as a general
source of distress by Van Maanen and Schein, who
have observed:

Individuals undergoing any organizational transition are in an anxiety-producing situation. In the main, they are more or less motivated to reduce this anxiety by learning the functional and social requirements of their newly assumed role as quickly as possible. The sources of this anxiety are many. To wit, psychological tensions are prompted no doubt by the feelings of loneliness and isolation that are associated initially with a new location in an organization as well as the performance anxieties a person may have when assuming new duties. Gone also is the learned social situation with its established and comfortable routines for handling interaction and predicting the responses of others to oneself. Thus stress is likely because newcomers to a particular organizational role will initially feel a lack of identification with the various activities observed to be going on about them. Needless to say, different kinds of transitions will invoke different levels of anxiety, but any passage from the familiar to the less familiar will create some difficulties for the individual moving on.[32]

Ample testimony to support these observations are the reports of men and women who have moved into sex-atypical occupations. They, more than others who make occupational or organizational moves, have made a transition from the familiar to the less familiar, to a position where there have been few or no others like them before. Such a situation lacks the security of learned routine, of shared expectations, and is in fact an acute case of the "lack of identification" that these authors consider part of all new organizational situations. Lack of identification, dissimilarity, isolation—these are characteristic of the experiences described by female lawyers and male nurses, experiences that seem to have been associated with the tension and anxiety described by Van Maanen and Schein.

Both the process of job change (transition) undergone by men and women who move into sex-atypical jobs and the actual occupancy of those jobs (transposition) can be viewed as sources of anxiety or distress. That occupying such a position would be a source of distress for individuals was predicted twenty years ago by Everett Hughes. Hughes anticipated the "dilemmas and contradictions of status" faced by those who entered occupations where others like them had not been. Such a phenomenon, which Hughes saw as a consequence of America's opportunity for individual mobility, would evoke certain kinds of difficulty for the "newcomers" and for the "old hands," those whose position as members of the occupational group had been traditional or predictable. Hughes proposed that the appearance of a new kind of person would constitute a "status contradiction," a violation of expectations about the characteristics usually associated with that particular position.[33] This contradiction would, in turn, lead to a dilemma for the new member of the occupational group and as such would require *perceptual, attitudinal, and behavioral adaptations for both newcomer and old hands.* Such adaptations, Hughes proposed, might take many forms; and they could influence group process, both between members and between newcomers and old hands. Hughes went so far as to predict a long-term position of "marginality" for the person in a position of status contradiction.

Hughes's predictions about the consequences of American social and occupational mobility have been at least partly confirmed some twenty years later. These days, because of governmental interventions as well as changing attitudes, more and different employees are entering work situations where they are the first or second of their kind. While Hughes anticipated that these new arrivals would have some difficulty in becoming members of their work groups, a more recent commentator, Kanter, has developed more specific expectations about the role and position of the male or female newcomer to a job usually occupied by the other sex. From this perspective, when the New Type employee enters a new work group, that person undergoes universal experiences based on his or her uniqueness in that group setting. Because of a visible difference in *one* characteristic—sex—this person becomes a "token" and is viewed differently by other members of that group, which in turn affects his or her behavior, affect, and attitudes in the group. The position of the "token" person then has more to do with the contrast between that person and the rest of the group than with the sex or color of that individual. Such a view highlights the structural aspects of the work situation as determinants of attitudes and behaviors for both newcomers and old hands.[34]

Kanter has developed more specific predictions about the enactment of the token's role in the work group. Because of heightened visibility, the token person experiences self-consciousness and performance pressure. The visible contrast between the token and the rest of the group continues as a reminder of the token's exclusion from the dominant group and his or her difference from its members. Finally, because of a tendency toward stereotyping, a form of "role encapsulation" can occur. The token moves into a slot, a position identified with his or her subgroup, and ends up playing out a particular role or part in group life. This role may or may not be appropriate to the token's unique characteristics, but it does match some aspect of the stereotype about the token's difference from the rest of the group.

These predictions apply to the experience of the New Type person in the work group and also to the work group experience over time. Van Maanen and Schein's predictions about transitions and their attached anxiety pertain to the entry of the New Type into the work group, to the period of time when new group members are considered for membership by "old hands." According to Van Maanen and Schein's proposition, the transition of the New Type employee into the new work group should be more distressing than that of the Same Type employee in the same situation, on three bases: the move is from familiar to very unfamiliar; there is a heightened lack of identification with members of the surrounding work situation; and the New Type moves across more organizational and occupational boundaries than the Same

Type who moves into a new position. For all these reasons, both transition and transposition for the male and female New Types are probably more distressing than those experiences for Same Types.

What is expected to result from these kinds of differences is some form of "stress," some kind of psychological, physiological, attitudinal, or behavioral difference between the work experience of New Types and Same Types. We might also expect to find some differences in the quality of work group relationships, in the quality of work life in general, most particularly when the New Types first begin their jobs. At the entry time all the dimensions that make their work experiences different are highlighted. Especially at this time, the attitudes and behavior of both the new person and the work group may be exaggerated.

Along with different feelings about work and co-workers, men or women who have made transitions into a job typically associated with the other sex, and who are currently occupying a minority position in a work group predominantly composed of the other sex, may have different feelings about themselves than those who match the sex-type of their work groups. Generally, people do view and evaluate themselves and their competencies in an interpersonal context. Certain kinds of self-view are influenced by the immediate situation and by those in the setting with whom one makes personal comparison. If the others are different, this difference appears to affect individual perceptions of "fit" with the job and the social situation and with perceptions and evaluations of competence and self-esteem. Individuals often choose similar others for comparison; such choice serves an important purpose. As one psychologist has noted, "When another is seen as similar to the self, he places a stamp of legitimacy on one's conduct or appearance . . . [whereas] encountering an individual whose characteristics differ from one's own may initiate a process of self-questioning and doubt."[35] Does the entry of a man or woman into a situation predominantly occupied by the other sex stimulate personal questioning and self-doubt? Psychologists have also observed that individuals do not compare themselves to others on the basis of one ability or characteristic at a time; instead they take a more global view of themselves to derive a general feeling of self-esteem.[36] If such is the case, then individuals who enter a group of others different from them, in a situation where this difference is exaggerated, may make this difference the basis for a more global change in self-esteem than might be predicted from comparison of one characteristic or another. Perhaps the different man or woman experiences less specific confidence about himself or herself in the job and perhaps a more global diminution of self-esteem as a result of being in the midst of different others.

Another element of the worker's entry into a new work situation is his or her reception by others in the work group. Again empirical evidence has suggested that we generally like others who most resemble us; conversely those who seem most different will be most disdainful of us and our abilities.[37] This evidence supports Hughes's prediction that the minority person will be treated as a stranger, perhaps viewed with suspicion, perhaps not appreciated, perhaps not liked or included.

Research Directions and Questions: Summary

What then have these reports, theories, and statistics led us to expect of a situation where men and women have moved into sex-atypical work situations? At the beginning of this discussion I outlined a number of social, economic, and political characteristics that form the background for the individual experience. I began with recognition of (1) a division of labor by sex; (2) the sex-typing of jobs; (3) differences between cultures and time periods in the specifics of sex-type for jobs; (4) the segregation of occupations by sex; (5)

the implications of segregation by sex for sex differences in work force participation; (6) implications of
segregation by sex for sex differences in individual occupational choice, selection, placement, access to vertical mobility and to influence within organizations. Within this context I elaborated some of the more individualized theories about personal responses to difference and change.

Difference and change are the underlying themes of this study. I have assumed that passages into and out of jobs are stressful changes for individuals, that entering a job where one is different from those currently and previously in the job, where one is not "expected" to be, is a greater change than is usually associated with entering a new job. On this basis, then, I suggest that a systematic study will highlight differences in the work experiences of men and women who enter sex-atypical work situations (New Types) and men and women who enter work situations where their peers are the same sex (Same Types).

One sidelight of this basic research pertains to my assumption about equivalent experiences for men and women New Types in their entry and occupancy of sex-atypical jobs. In most respects it makes sense to assume equivalence based on the theoretical presumptions about changes involving the concepts of transition and transposition central to this work. Yet there is enough evidence about differences in prestige and status between male and female occupations in this culture to suggest a subsidiary focus—on the differences between the experiences of men and women New Types. If the issues of status and prestige differences between male and female jobs are not salient, then there should be little evidence of difference between the men and women and their experiences as New Type members of work situations. If the issues of status and prestige are meaningful, then there should be some evidence of this meaning in the outcomes of a study.

With this background I developed a set of research questions that addressed three central concerns. The first focused on a systematic comparison of the work responses of New Type and Same Type employees in a particular work setting. The second focused on comparisons between the responses of male and female New Types to their work. A third set of questions explored some of the issues and themes that characterized the work experience of a group of men and women who had entered sex-atypical jobs.

Through the systematic comparison of a group of men and women in sex-atypical jobs with a group of men and women in sex-typical jobs, I intended to address the following questions.

1. Are there differences in *feelings* about the work experience described by New Type and Same Type employees? Through a focus on affective states, I was interested in differences between the two groups in terms of salient affective dimensions based on theories about difference and change. Are there differences between the two groups in the affective response to the work situation, as reflected in work satisfaction or satisfaction with supervisor, co-workers, pay, and promotion opportunities? Are there differences in their feelings about pressures to perform? Are there differences between the two groups in the tension and anxiety they experience in relation to their jobs, as expressed through reports of psychological or somatic symptoms or in terms of rates of absence from work?

2. Are there differences in self-perception with regard to work described by the New Type and Same Type employees? Do the two groups view themselves differently in terms of their "fit" with the job, performance on the job, confidence in their work abilities, social "fit" with others on the job, and clarity of a future in this organization?

3. Are there differences in the amount of "social support"[38] available from bosses and peers described by the New Type and Same Type employees? Social

support in the work environment has been described as an important factor in alleviating work-related stress. When the New Type employee moves into an unfamiliar situation, the comparative availability of social support from others in the work environment should be important.

4. Are there differences in supervisors' perceptions and evaluations of the New Type and Same Type employees? Do supervisors perceive the New Type employees differently from the Same Types, who are "expected" members of a particular sex-typed job? Are there differences on the same perceptual dimensions addressed to the employees themselves: in "appropriateness" or "fit" with the job, in the supervisor's perception of the employee's self-confidence, of the employee's "fit" with the work group, of the employee's future in the organization, and in the evaluation of the employee's work performance?

In addition to the systematic comparisons generated by previous work and predictions about change and stress, I also proposed a set of exploratory questions that probed descriptive material about personal experiences. These questions included general clusters of inquiry such as these.

What kinds of experience did the New Type men and women describe, in general, about their entry into the work setting?

Are there any clear patterns or themes in these experiences related to sex differences, length of time on the job, or presence of other New Type employees at the time of the employee's entry into the current job?

How did the Same Types describe the entry experiences of the New Types? Are there areas of similarity or difference in the description that pertain to sex differences, length of time in the job, or demographic characteristics of the observer?

How did the Same Type describe their own reactions to the introduction of New Types to their work settings? Are there differences in the personal reports that pertain to sex differences and length of time in position?

Beginnings: My Job

In general I developed a study about the effects of change—of transitions into unfamiliar organizational situations and occupancy of unexpected occupational positions. How were these changes experienced by those who made them? How were they viewed by those who did not make them but whose work groups were changed with the arrival of newcomers? What did these kinds of changes *mean* to the men and women whose lives were touched by them? These feelings and meanings occurred in a social context characterized by norms and expectations about who belonged where, about which jobs were "right" for which sex, which person. The pressure of social change had been affecting some of those norms and expectations, since men and women were moving into new situations. Still, these moves were enacted in a changing environment, an environment still characterized by attitudes and expectations well rooted in history and tradition. Were attitudes and expectations actually changing along with the changes enacted by individuals? The questions were clear; the development of meaningful answers was another story.

3 STARTING OUT:
METHODS AND MAIN FINDINGS

The questions I had raised to begin this study were shared in large part by an organization with which I had previous professional contact. Because the organization was interested in learning about the work experiences of men and women who had recently moved into sex-atypical jobs, the site and setting for research were easily located. A more complicated task was the actual development of the study, with its attendant decisions about methodology and research strategy. These decisions became more complicated when the process of developing the research turned up evidence that influenced my original questions and, in turn, what I actually learned through the study. In other words, the research process itself changed the shape of the study and my interests, paralleling the changing situation I was attempting to describe.

As important as the report of procedures and methods, then, is a report of process and history. So as not to interrupt the pace, I report most of the research process in the epilogue, where I consider the mutual influences among procedures and processes. The epilogue also provides an opportunity to speculate about the difficulties of this approach and register some thoughts about the reluctance to acknowledge, appreciate, and report changing pace in traditional research documents. The report of the study shows the importance of surprises to the direction and outcome of this project. As surprises became data, the questions and outcomes changed shape and direction.

Beginnings: When and Where

BCO is a company located in northeastern United States. As of December 1975 the company employed approximately 13,000 people, about 52 percent male and 48 percent female. Of the approximately 3,500 management employees in the company, approximately 67 percent were male and 33 percent were female. Of the approximately 9,500 non-management employees in the company, 47 percent were male and 53 percent were female.

In late 1975 when I was first introduced to the company, it had been engaged in an Affirmative Action program for about two years. At that time personnel managers were beginning to ask about the individual and organizational implications of Affirmative Action policies, practices, and programs for those whose work placements had been directly affected. One of their main interests was in men and women who had taken sex-atypical nonmanagement positions, an interest I shared.

With the company's interest and support I chose to study the situations of these nonmanagement men and women, follow up on their experiences in the job, look at their sense of fit with the job and the social environment, and compare these work experiences with those of a comparable group of men and women in positions considered typical for their sex. The study was to encompass a set of nonmanagement jobs that were then occupied by both men and women but had been considered typical of one sex in the past.

The complexities and subtleties of carrying out this research are described in detail and with commentary in the epilogue. For now, though, it is important to know something about the research history because it did influence the study's findings. In brief, during the research I learned that one of the jobs I had selected for study was being modified through the introduction of technology and that employees in that job were being informed of proposed cutbacks in the labor force. This "male" job was one into which a large proportion (26 percent) of women had been integrated. Originally I had planned to study this job as the single "male" job in my study and to compare it with one "female" job in a simple two-way comparison. Once I learned about the imminent changes in the "male" job, I had to expand the number and array of jobs in the study so that this significant source of change and stress operating on one job

would not unduly influence my study. For this reason,
I selected eight nonmanagement jobs for inclusion in
the study, four typically "female" and four typically
"male." (Appendix A lists the jobs selected and the
relative proportions of men and women in them in
1974, 1975, and 1976.) From these eight jobs I selected
a sample of 100 men and women who were interviewed in the summer of 1976.

Beginnings: Who

Aggregate information about these 100 employees
provides a general introduction to them as a group.
More specific characteristics will emerge through
group profiles and through the words and feelings of
the individuals. The average age of the participants
was 27.9 years. Most employees reported that their
parents had less education than they had: the average
parent did not complete high school. The mean level
of educational attainment for these 100 employees
was high school graduation plus some form of technical training or some college. The general educational level of the sample group and their parents
indicates a background in the lower middle class.

Included in the study were occupants of eight different kinds of jobs. All the female sex-typed jobs
were described as clerical positions. All four jobs involved some form of recording or reporting, filing,
and some calculations. The jobs did not require sec-
retarial skills such as typing or stenographic work,
although such skills would have been an asset. The
job with the largest number of occupants in this study
(19 men and 19 women) involved both clerical work
and contact with clients or "the public." I have labeled
this job the clerical-service job, since it encompassed
the two basic functions of clerical and service responsibilities. The other clerical positions I have labeled
clerical-support jobs because they maintained an
internal focus, serving as resources to other members
of the company. Their functions were often related to

information collection, classification, and compilation, sometimes for the use of technicians and sometimes for input to the computer. Although all these jobs were "pink-collar" positions, typically held by women, and in the same category for pay, they presented quite different situations to employees. Each job had its pressures and cross pressures. Those in the clerical-service job were subject to conflicting pressures from clients and company; the pressure to serve was in constant conflict with the pressure to maintain adequate records and keep the bills paid. The cross pressures for the support people came more from the different "bosses" to whom they were responsible. Their own supervisors' needs were at times in conflict with the requests of the technicians, a difficult situation for some individuals. The work required considerable and constant attention in order not to fall behind. All the clerical jobs specified a total of twelve months for training.

Two of the male jobs were blue-collar. These two jobs were differentiated by the skill levels they required, by their position in the organizational hierarchy, and by pay. Thus I call one the senior crafts job and the other the junior crafts job. There were other important differences between these two jobs, although the jobs were often done in the same setting and were part of the same function in the company. The junior crafts job had traditionally been an entry-level position for many male employees; now females held 26 percent of these jobs. This job involved a lot of physical movement, manual dexterity, and much tinkering with machinery and equipment.

The senior crafts jobs engaged similar skills but required more sophistication about machinery and repairs; this sophistication was usually the result of having previously held the junior crafts jobs. In addition to the basic activities assigned to the junior craft job, the senior craft person had more complex responsibilities, including more direct repair and mainte-

nance work. This person was also assigned the lifting
of heavy packages, one characteristic that distinguished this job from the junior craft job. There was a major difference in the training time required for each position. The junior craft job required one week of formal classroom training and about eight months of on-the-job training, a total of nine months to learn the job. The senior craft job required eight months in the classroom and four years of on-the-job training, a total learning time of five years.

The other two male jobs were the gray-collar jobs—high-level technical positions that involve skill and responsibility for equipment planning. Because they involved no actual contact with equipment, these jobs were not blue-collar jobs. They were not white-collar jobs because they were not in the management ranks. And they were not pink-collar jobs since they were typically associated with men. These jobs combined a number of characteristics of managerial and technical work; they involved technical expertise for planning and development, as well as some independent and some collaborative decision making about equipment. The jobs were differentiated again by their level in the organization, by pay, and by their responsibilities. The junior technician job was lower in the hierarchy and offered less pay, but it was considered a prerequisite for the senior technician job. Often junior and senior technicians worked together on projects, but the transition between the two positions took time and effort. Training for the junior technician job had been fairly well developed by the company and was accompanied by specific performance criteria. Overall training for the junior technician position took about nine months for the initial work and about twelve to eighteen months on the job. The senior technician position relied on skills and training acquired in the junior position and thus offered a short (one-week) classroom training period coupled with a year of on-the-job training.

Of all these jobs, the one with the highest position in the organizational hierarchy and the highest was the senior technician job, followed by the junior technician, the senior crafts job, and the junior crafts job. All the clerical jobs were lower in the hierarchy and paid less than the first four, although there was some overlap in pay ranges between the junior craft job and the clerical positions.[1]

Beginnings: How

The study engaged 100 nonmanagement employees in one company for an interview and questionnaire session of one and one-half hours. (All instruments are included in appendix B.) Fifty of the study participants were male and female occupants of eight sex-atypical jobs; the other fifty participants were male and female sex-typical occupants of the same jobs. All participants were asked about reactions to their jobs, expectations about the future, and feelings about fit with the job and with others present on the job. I asked about their views of their own abilities, skills, and the organizational picture of social support on the job from supervisors and peers. All participants were asked for permission to contact their supervisors with a questionnaire, and all agreed. The questions that differed for employees in sex-atypical jobs versus those in sex-typical jobs focused on the experiences of moving into a new situation. These questions were descriptive of feeling, behavior, and attitude, often in retrospect. Questions asked of sex-typical employees addressed their reactions to the entry of New Types to their work situations and sought descriptions of feelings, behavior, and attitude, often in retrospect. All the participants at one time or another had been exposed to the impending or actual arrival of a New Type, and so could speak of their and others' reactions. These conversations, whether quantified as scales or maintained as qualitative verbal data, became the basis for data analysis and subsequent understanding in light of the organizational context.

To provide a better picture of the people who participated in this study, I have described some of their characteristics by group, so that similarities and differences can be appreciated. Some of the characterizations make more sense once the study is explicated, but the basic differences between groups should be clear from the beginning. The following profiles of the four groups in this study outline their shared themes and notable characteristics. Who is the "typical" employee in this study? How might she or he react to and perceive the current work situation? What are the concerns about taking the present job, and what are the hopes and dreams for the future?

Male Same Type

The male employee in a sex-typical job holds one of two nonmanagement jobs: craft or technical. He is about $29\frac{1}{2}$ years old, has held his job for almost four years, and has a high school degree with some additional specialized or college training. If he is not in the junior craft job, the male Same Type employee tends to be satisfied with his work, pay, co-workers, supervisor, and opportunities for promotion. But even if he is comfortable with his position, he tends to feel that women currently have better chances to move ahead in the company, a situation that just "isn't fair." He has mixed feelings about the entry of women into his job and work situations. At first he felt that women were "just there to meet some quota" and were often "rejecting, would turn a cold shoulder." As time went on, though, he notes that "they're readily accepted now. Now that women are proving they can do it, we accept them right away." Acceptance of women is often accompanied by some concern, especially at the lower-level jobs, about the male employee's own future possibilities in the company.

Female Same Type

The female sex-typical employee occupies a clerical position. If she had had another choice, she would have been a nurse or a teacher, since she likes to work with people. She is about $26\frac{1}{2}$ years old, a high school graduate, and has been in her job about three years. She feels in general that "it's a good company to get into." In general, she is satisfied with her pay, supervisors, co-workers, and opportunities for promotion, although she may express dissatisfaction with the content of her work. If she is in a clerical-service job, she may complain about the pressure from the job: "No one tells you about the amount of clerical work, and you start out expecting to be helpful. There's so much pressure from the paper work that you can't be helpful." In general, the woman in a sex-typical position believes that men have more opportunities for future positions in management, despite the promises of EEOC; and she often believes that men have taken clerical positions like hers to move ahead in the company, as stepping-stones. If she herself has ambition, it is frequently to move up one or two steps. Rarely does she consider herself a candidate for a management position.

Female New Type

She is about $29\frac{1}{2}$ years old and has held her job for about $2\frac{1}{2}$ years. She is a high school graduate, with some additional training. If she were not in this job, she would be in a job outdoors, doing physical work or working with her hands; she might be a medical technician. If she is in a craft position, she has usually worked for the company in another job, often at a lower level, and considers her present job an improvement over that one. If she is in one of the higher-level technical jobs, she most often worked into it through clerical positions. If she is in a technical job, she reports an easier beginning in the job, with less teasing, and more present satisfaction than her coun-

terparts in craft jobs. If she is in a craft job, she found
starting somewhat difficult and still finds people look- ing to see whether she has made a mistake in her work. In general she sees limited opportunity for herself in the company, though that may mean that she sees limited opportunity for everyone because of the over- all lack of jobs. She has not talked with anyone about moving up and is currently grateful for the kind of work and the salary offered by her current job. She is more satisfied with her salary than other employees in the study and is generally satisfied with her work as well.

Male New Type

He is about $26\frac{1}{2}$ years old and has been in the present job for a year and a half. He took his current job as a stepping-stone and sees himself moving beyond it into a management position. Had he not taken the clerical position, he would have pursued police work, land- scaping, accounting, or electronics work. He maintains an open view about the future and names a number of higher-level nonmanagement or management posi- tions as possible options. Despite the number of op- tions mentioned, he still believes that women have better or equal chances for future positions in the company, a situation that he generally decries. His feelings about the job vary. Although as a male clerical he often shares the complaints of his female counter- parts about job pressure and tension, he sees the con- dition as temporary, since he intends to rise from that job into another in the organization. His initial experi- ences in his job were generally positive; and he notes a welcoming attitude on the part of female peers and supervisors. On the whole his present work experi- ences are positive, and when they are not, they are brightened by optimism about the future.

In addition to these profiles, one important charac- teristic differed among the four groups of partici- pants: length of time in the job. Although the overall average time on the job was 31.3 months, individual groups ranged from 23.7 months for all the New Types to 38.8 for all the Same Types. The male New Types were in their jobs for the shortest period (18 months average), followed by the female New Types (22 months), the female Same Types (31.8 months), and the male Same Types (45.8) months. This difference indicates more variation in length of time in the job than I had originally intended. Because of recession and employment difficulties, it was impossible to select a sample of 100 employees who were comparably new to their jobs.

Another important characteristic of the sample pertains to choice of or assignment to the current job. Whether the job was occupied by choice or by assignment might affect the employees' affective response to the work situation. When asked whether they had chosen their current job, employees reported as shown in table 1.

Among the New Type employees, 90 percent said they had chosen to be in their present jobs, while 10 percent said they had been assigned to them. Among the Same Types, 94 percent had chosen to be in this job, while 6 percent were assigned to them. Since most study participants felt that they had chosen their current positions, I assume that the effect of choice or assignment is not a major influence on the study's findings. Still there may be important differences in their reasons for taking their jobs. I examine these differences in a later chapter.

First Findings

The combination of original research questions with additional organizational realities presented a challenge for data analysis. On the one hand, my initial questions were based on simple comparisons between the fifty New Type and fifty Same Type employees and were developed from an understanding about the sex-typing of occupations coupled with predictions about stress and change. From this per-

Table 1

Job Choice or Assignment

	New Types		Same Types	
	Female	Male	Female	Male
Choice	24	21	24	23
Assignment	1	4	1	2
Total	25	25	25	25

spective I predicted that change into and within a sex-atypical position would lead to differences between New Type and Same Type employees in their work-related feelings and perceptions. I also predicted differences in terms of supervisors' perceptions of their abilities, their fit with the job, and the quality of their work.

As the project developed, I identified other potentially stressful conditions as a result of my immersion in the organization and the research. The most obvious additional candidate for a stress condition was the threat of job loss or change, a condition that affected one of the jobs studied ($n = 24$). Simple group-by-group comparisons that ignored the effect of this job on sample members could not tell the complete story about differences between New Types and Same Types. Similarly, other characteristics of the work situation and potential interactions between them had to be included in a realistic approach to data analysis.

To meet the multiple interests of this analytic focus, I used a twofold strategy. Initially I went through the basic comparisons between the two major groups and followed these comparisons with more elaborate and sophisticated analyses that took into account the multiple independent conditions in this work situation and the interactions between these conditions. These analyses were useful because they matched the complexity of the organizational situation and indicated the relative importance of organizational conditions affecting these work situations.

Comparing the Groups: New Types, Same Types

For the initial group comparisons, the t-test for difference between means was applied, with the criterion for significance established at $p < 0.10$ for a two-tailed test. Appendix C lists the variable means, standard deviations, t-values, and probabilities for these comparisons.

The first comparisons were based on the research questions proposed and outlined in chapter 1. They pertained to differences between New Types and Same Type employees on measures of their feelings about work, supervisor, pay, promotion, and co-workers; affective responses in terms of tension, pressure, and anxiety in relation to their jobs, as expressed through reports of psychological or somatic symptoms or in terms of absence from work. I also looked at differences in self-perception with regard to work; in terms of fit with the job and social fit with others on the job; self-view of performance on the job, confidence in work abilities, and clarity about a future in this organization.

Results of the initial comparisons based on these questions were limited to the measurement of the effect of the single condition (occupancy of a New Type or Same Type job) on the important outcome characteristics. These comparisons show minimal difference between the two comparison groups. Among the few differences that are significant, one is positive for employees in sex-typical jobs. In general their supervisors see them as more confident about their work $[t(98) = 2.22, p < 0.03]$.

Contrary to my expectations, differences between the two groups of employees emphasize the more positive aspects of occupying a sex-atypical position. The New Types consider themselves somewhat better matched to their jobs $[t(98) = 1.67, p < 0.09]$, anticipate clearer job futures $[t(98) = 2.22, p < 0.03]$, and are more satisfied with their work than employees in sex-typical positions $[t(98) = 2.57, p <$

0.01]. Thus the most dramatic difference between the two groups is their response to work, as measured by the JDI subscale that measures satisfaction with work per se.[2]

Satisfaction with work and "fit" with the job are two responses to the work situation (one affective and one self-perceptual) that I did not expect to be part of the New Types' work experience. Although expectations about change and stress suggested predictions of more discomfort for the New Types, the reverse was true. When there were significant differences between the two groups, the New Types were generally more positive.

The verbatim comments offered by employees echoed the first round of statistical findings, surprising as they were. There was a pronounced difference between the two groups of employees in the quality of comments they made about their work, providing some indication of what made their work enjoyable. Men and women in sex-atypical jobs mentioned specific features of their work.

I like to work with my hands.

I like the chance to move around; to sit in one place all day would drive me crazy.

I like the variety. New things are happening all the time.

Even though the mass of paperwork was awesome, and I was never tied to a desk before, I like this job. I like helping other people.

Men and women in jobs typical for their sex also made positive comments, but they had more to do with the work environment than with the work itself. They were more likely to comment about benefits, atmosphere, pay, and hours than about the work itself.

Although the initial univariate analyses suggested positive personal responses to occupying sex-atypical jobs, this suggestion needed refinement because of all the other factors operating in this organizational situation. The *t*-test results cannot be attributed unambiguously to differences between employees in sex-typical and sex-atypical jobs. A more effective approach would be a simultaneous consideration of features of the job that were hypothesized to contribute to work-related affect, perception, and behavior as well as the relative and combined influences of job features on these outcomes. For instance, at this point in the analysis we knew nothing about the relative effects of job type (and concurrent technological change attached to the eight jobs) and length of time on the job, about length of time on the job and traditional or nontraditional occupancy, or about the combined effect of length of time in a particular job on the designated outcome measures. All these factors might influence the way an individual feels about his or her work.

Multiple Regression Analysis

Multiple regression analysis provides a convenient approach to examine explanatory variables in a limited number of combinations and their relationships, both singly and in combination, to a dependent variable.[3] Although regression analysis affords only speculation about causality, it does allow us to consider a complete set of independent variables as possible explainers or predictors of a particular outcome. In this research the use of multiple regression analysis was determined by a need to probe the initial findings and to pursue theoretical implications. Empirically it was important to understand the relative effect of different stress conditions on employee response, both singly and in combination. We had identified at least two characteristics as stress conditions in this work situation: sex-atypical job occupancy and, subsequently, occupancy of a job vulnerable to changes in work force membership because of changes in technology. Each of these characteristics conformed to the previous identification of change as a stress condition. A crucial theoretical and empirical question centered on the combined presence of these two stress conditions. Would they compete or combine in their influence on individual work-related affect? Theoretically as well, the research situation provided the opportunity to look at issues not previously considered in other work or stress: the positive sequellae attached to stress and the comparative and combined effects of different environmental stress conditions.

For these reasons the selection of individual criterion and outcome variables was based on a mix of empirical and theoretical motives. The criteria for inclusion of variables in the regression analysis were (1) original theoretical importance: sex-typical/sex-atypical job occupancy (designated as a stress condition); sex of occupant; availability of social support from supervisor and peers; sex match of employee and supervisor; (2) characteristics that seemed to be of empirical importance: type of job (designated as a stress condition for the junior craft job), and length of time in the job. Also included were interactions between these variables: length of time in a particular job; sex-atypical occupancy of a particular job (designated as a stress condition for the junior craft job).

The Full Model: Work Satisfaction

Through this analysis we proposed that the combined effects of the following variables and their interactions would explain variation in work satisfaction among employees. (The full model for the regression analysis on work satisfaction is included as appendix D.)

1
Match of worker sex to sex-type of job. Are Same Type employees more satisfied than New Types?

2
Sex of worker. How much does being male or female influence work satisfaction?

3
Sex match of employee and supervisor (match and non-match). Is there a difference in satisfaction with work between employees who are sex matched with supervisors and those who are not?

4
Kind of job (five categories that represent the eight jobs included in the sample). One job, the junior craft job, is identified as a potential detractor from work satisfaction. Are employees in this job ($n = 24$) less satisfied than employees in other jobs? Does this characteristic affect overall work satisfaction?

5
Social support from supervisor. Does a report of high supervisory social support affect variation in work satisfaction?

6
Social support from peers (two categories, high and low). Does a report of high social support from peers affect variation in work satisfaction?

7
Length of time in the job (quantitative, number of months). Does the length of time on the job affect variation in work satisfaction?

8
Combined effects of conditions 1–7 are measured as interactions of
a. Length of time in job and kind of job (five categories).
b. Length of time in job for sex-typical/sex-atypical employees (two quantitative categories).
c. Kind of job and sex match or sex nonmatch of employee (five categories).

The Final Model: Results

With all these variables and their interactions included in the full model equation, $R^2 = 0.546$. $\bar{R}^2 = 0.423$. The variables in the equation singly and in combination accounted for over 50 percent of the variance in work satisfaction.

Use of the backward elimination technique reduced the number of variables from fifteen to six. We then had an R^2 of 0.496 and an $\bar{R}^2$ of 0.462. In the final model we have lost very little raw explanatory power (R^2), and corrected explanatory power ($\bar{R}^2$) has improved. All variables remaining in the final equation had significant F values. Table 2 shows the results of the final model.

Three kinds of information can be interpreted from this final equation and its values. First, this combination of variables has overall explanatory power in relation to worker satisfaction. This set of variables provides a better combination of parsimony and explanatory power in relation to work satisfaction than any other combination drawn from the original set in the model. Second, we can make some comparisons between variable categories, which provide more refined information. Third, through the computation of another statistic, *usefulness*, we can discern the relative explanatory power of each of the variables left in the equation.

With regard to the overall explanatory power of the final equation, note that an R^2 of 0.49 is a high value to be obtained in a field study, especially one that used predominantly organizational and situational variables to explain an attitude.

Among the variables that did survive and now make up the final equation, what meaning can be attributed to their presence and to the values attached to them?

Table 2
Work Satisfaction: Final Model

Variable	b	s.e.(b)	Beta	F
Social Support from Supervisor	9.05	1.92	0.369	22.2
Employee-Supervisor Sex Match	− 6.2	2.51	−0.250	5.99
Job Type 1 Clerical Service	−14.9	2.73	−0.595	30.2
Job Type 5 Junior Craft	−21.8	3.18	−0.761	46.9
Sex-Atypicals in Job Type 1 (Males)	12.2	3.61	0.391	11.4
Sex-Atypicals in Job Type 5 (Females)	12.7	4.34	0.337	8.6

Constant 36.54

Because of the dummy coding, comparisons can be made between variable categories, based on the *b* values. Employees who report high social support from their supervisors are, on the average, more satisfied with their jobs than those who report low social support, the difference being 9.05 points on the JDI work satisfaction scale. Again, employees of a different sex from their supervisors are less satisfied with their work than those who are the same sex as their supervisors, the difference being 6.02 points on the JDI work satisfaction scale.

When the relative effects of occupancy of one job or another are compared, the presence in the final equation of job type 1 (clerical-service) and job type 5 (junior craft) indicates that occupancy of these jobs explains some differences between employees in their satisfaction with their work. Based on our earlier categorical coding system, we are essentially comparing those in the clerical-service and the junior craft job with those in the senior technical job (job type 8) when we interpret the regression coefficients. Thus all clerical-service employees are expected to have JDI work scores about 15 points lower than all senior technicians (and to be that much more dissatisfied with their jobs). Still, the sex-atypical clerical-service person (male) reports JDI work scores 12 points higher than the female occupants of that job, in general. In the clerical-service job the work satisfaction of the sex-atypical employee is increased by his position. His JDI work score is still 3 points lower on the average than those of both males and females in the senior technician job.

All occupants of the junior craft job, the job most vulnerable to technological change and loss of work force, score about 22 points lower on the JDI work scale than senior technicians, although the sex-atypical junior crafts workers (females) score 12.7 points higher than the average junior craft score. The female junior craft workers are thus only 9 points lower on the JDI ($-21.8 + 12.7$) than the senior technicians as a group. Junior crafts persons are obviously less satisfied with their work than any other group of employees in the study; and this dissatisfaction affects both men and women, though to different extents.

From the different values of the variables in the final equation, we can use the usefulness statistics to examine the relative ability of each variable to explain variation in worker satisfaction. In a multiple regression analysis the *usefulness*[4] of a variable is the amount by which R^2 would drop if that variable were deleted from the model. Thus it is an incremental measure of that variable's importance. For the final equation the measures of usefulness shown in table 3 were computed.

What does this statistic indicate about the relative explanatory power of the surviving variables in relation to worker satisfaction? Among the surviving variables, the most potent source of variation in work satisfaction is occupancy of one job — junior crafts, the position most vulnerable to change. Inclusion of this job in the model contributes a large portion of what we know about variation in worker satisfaction (0.25 of a total of 0.49). Since each of the usefulness values represents the portion of variance explained that would be lost by elimination of that variable from the equation, about half of our understanding of satis-

Table 3
Measures of Usefulness

Variable	F	Usefulness
Social Support from Supervisor	22.2	0.12
Employee-Supervisor (Sex Match)	5.99	0.03
Job Type 1, Clerical-Service	30.2	0.16
Job Type 5, Junior Craft	46.9	0.25
New Type, Job Type 1 (Male Clerical Service)	11.4	0.06
New Type, Job Type 5 (Female Junior Craft)	8.6	0.05

faction would be unknown if the junior crafts person's job were not included in this explanatory model. On the other hand, we would have lost far less explanatory information if we had not included supervisor-employee sex match, which only contributes about 0.03 to the 0.49 total variance explained by the equation. Not knowing about the sex match of supervisor and employee would "cost" much less in terms of understanding satisfaction than not knowing about occupancy of the junior crafts job or of the clerical-service job, which contributed 0.16 to the 0.48 total.

The inclusion of social support from supervisor in the final equation indicates the importance of this attitude measure in relation to the dependent variable, which is also an attitude measure. Although common method variance (self-report) may account in part for their association, the other self-report measure in the original equation (peer support) did not survive the regression analysis procedure. Knowledge of the amount of social support from supervisor gives us 0.12 of the 0.48 of what we know about variance in satisfaction. In other words, not knowing about the amount of supervisor social support reported by the employee would take away about 25 percent of what we know about employee's work satisfaction. In comparison to this knowledge, knowing that the employee is a sex-atypical occupant of a job contributes far less to our understanding of differences in satisfaction. Still this knowledge enhances our understanding of differences in satisfaction more than sex match of employee and supervisor and far more than the variables that were dropped from the equation.

What do we learn about the data from the usefulness technique? The strongest contributions to understanding variation in employee satisfaction in this setting come not from the sources originally considered important but from specific empirical information about the employee's job. Knowing only that the employee was in the clerical-service or junior craft job would tell us more about his or her work satisfaction than would any other information about that employee.

Six variables contribute significantly to understanding differences in employee work satisfaction. The employee's sex, the match between employee sex and sex-type of job, and the length of time in the job were not among these variables, in contrast to what we anticipated. Instead the most prominent contributions to understanding are made by information about the occupancy of two jobs, one of which is vulnerable to changes in technology and loss of work force. These two situational characteristics, plus the nonmatch of employee-supervisor sex, detract from work satisfaction as measured by the JDI. Three other characteristics, social support from the supervisor and sex-atypical occupancy of the two least satisfying jobs, enhance work satisfaction. Whether enhancing or detracting from work satisfaction, each of these six characteristics contributes information to our understanding of work satisfaction in this situation.

Discussion

Results of the regression analysis on work satisfaction develop suggestions made by the original comparisons. The multiple regression procedure combined important criterion variables to propose an explanation of variation in worker satisfaction. These variables were drawn from theoretical prediction and empirical observation. This analysis has served as both a contextual tool and a conceptual stimulus; it has enabled us to examine the meaning of the phenomenon of original interest (the effect of person-job sex match on work satisfaction) within the context of the larger organization, with its multiple pressures and influences. In some sense we have put our theory in perspective in terms of competing influences on the worker. Acknowledging the effect of competing influences, we have been able to propose an explanatory model that accounts for a fairly high proportion of the variation in worker satisfaction. Without organizational information and the subsequent inclusion of job type and related interactions in the original equation, the analyses would have accounted for much less of the variation in the dependent variable. We would have known far less about what contributes to and detracts from worker satisfaction in this organization at this time.

This regression analysis has demonstrated statistically that the most salient determinants of worker satisfaction in this situation were occupancy of two particular jobs, whether one was a sex-atypical or sex-typical occupant of those jobs, social support from supervisor, and the sex match between employee and supervisor. We would not expect the more satisfied worker to hold the junior craft or clerical-service job or to receive high levels of social support from a supervisor of the same sex. The relatively dissatisfied worker might be an occupant of the junior craft or clerical-service job who would report low levels of social support from a supervisor not of the same sex. Again, sex-atypical occupancy of either of the least satisfying jobs appears to counteract the dissatisfaction inherent in the positions and to lead, in turn, to greater satisfaction with work for these positions.

The Paradox: Stress and Satisfaction

This analysis has explicated an unexpected but compelling relationship between combined stress conditions and work satisfaction. In this situation occupancy of a sex-atypical position (a stress condition) in jobs that are comparatively less satisfying appears to exert a positive effect on work satisfaction. In other words, employees whose work situation included two

stress conditions were more satisfied than those
whose work situation included only one stress condition, when that was the job itself.

How might these positive responses be explained?
One explanation may pertain to the way in which the
sex-atypical positions were chosen, since they were
not chosen on the basis of sex-specific expectations.
To choose a sex-atypical job, the employee had to use
criteria other than match of person/sex to job/sex type
as a basis for choice. Perhaps choices made on sex-
atypical bases are based more on self-perceived skills,
abilities, and preferences than on general expectations about who "belongs" in that job.

Some evidence to support this explanation comes
from the verbatim responses of the employees. When
asked about their work and its appropriateness for
them, the sex-typical and sex-atypical employees responded differently. The New Type employees more
often referred to specific characteristics of the work.

I like to work with my hands [female junior craft].

I like the chance to move around; to sit in one place all day
would drive me crazy [female junior craft].

I like the variety. New things are happening all the time
[male clerical-service].

Even though the mass of paperwork was awesome, and I
was never tied to a desk before, I like this job. I like helping
other people [male clerical-service].

Even though I thought that just doing a girl's job, just doing
clerical work, would be boring, it wasn't that way at all. I
enjoy it. It's a challenge. At the end of the week I feel as if
I've accomplished something [male clerical-service].

The responses of Same Type employees to interviewer probes were more oriented to context factors,
no matter what the respondent reported about "appropriateness," which was often positive.

I am satisfied with this job and don't think there is anything
around that would suit me better [female clerical-service].

The pay, benefits, and hours are good [female clerical-service].

The company benefits can't be beat [female clerical-service].

When there was negative affect about the person's match with the job, there were more complaints about the work climate from the Same Types, especially those in the clerical-service job.

I don't like the atmosphere here; there's too much pressure and tension [female clerical-service].

There's not enough time to do the clerical work and be helpful to the customers too [female clerical-service].

We don't have enough time to do all that we are supposed to do. I expected variety; but there is too much routine here [female clerical-service].

Unlike the New Types, the sex-typical employees in clerical-service jobs rarely mentioned specific qualities or characteristics of their jobs that they especially liked.

Despite the slight but significant difference between the two groups in terms of the scale measuring perceived fit with their job, there is a clear difference in the quality of response to probe questions about the job. The New Type men and women employees expressed far more work-related detail about and more specific points of attachment in their jobs.

The JDI work satisfaction subscale reflects affect similar to that measured by study scales and amplified by verbatim comments. The work subscale asks the respondent to describe his or her job by expressing agreement or disagreement with a list of descriptive adjectives. The checklist includes specific work-related characteristics; some correspond directly to the words of our sex-atypical respondents about their jobs: fascinating, satisfying, challenging, gives sense of accomplishment, useful. On the other hand, the negative descriptors echo the comments of the sex-typical employees: routine, boring, tiresome, simple, endless. The match between interview language and the instrument's key words is noticeable and reflects the significant difference between the sex-typical and sex-atypical employees in terms of their satisfaction with work as expressed in the JDI $[t(98) = 2.57, p < 0.01]$.

Choosing a job on the basis of a personal attribute other than sex may be a particularly effective mode for attracting individual abilities and skills to the appropriate job. Or, it may be that all the employees in sex-atypical positions were more "challengeable" than those in the sex-typical positions.

Stress, Pressure, and Satisfaction

Another potential source of influence on work satisfaction may be the amount of effort and commitment required to get involved with the job, to do the job well, or to do the job at all. We have some evidence on this question, elicited by questions pertaining to the original discussion of the token position.

From a theory about the token position, we predicted that the New Types would feel more pressure to do their jobs well than the Same Types would feel or report. This prediction was accurate, to a dramatic extent. There is a significant difference between these two sets of workers in their experience of extra pressure to do the job especially well $[t(98) = 21.2, p < 0.000)$. The origins of these feelings are discussed in a subsequent chapter; here I shall discuss their impact.

If the New Type employees felt pressure to do their jobs especially well, such pressures may have led to greater effort at the job, then to more involvement, and subsequently to more satisfaction derived from that effort and involvement. Perhaps the New Types, in feeling more pressure to do their work well, worked harder and became more committed to the work itself. This interpretation of connection between pressure, effort, involvement, and satisfaction corresponds to Locke's emphasis on work satisfaction.[5]

In summarizing the vast literature on causal factors in job satisfaction, Locke first focused on the work itself. He grouped the facets of work that have been found to be causally related to satisfaction as examples of "mental challenge." Specific characteristics that pertain to work satisfaction include "opportunity to use one's valued skills and abilities; opportunity for new learning; creativity; variety; difficulty; amount of work; responsibility; non-arbitrary pressure for performance; control over work methods and work place (autonomy); job enrichment; . . . and complexity."[6]

When the men and women in sex-atypical positions in this study described their work, they referred far more frequently to characteristics known to be causally related to work satisfaction than men and women in traditional positions. For example, "the opportunity to use one's skills and abilities" and "the opportunity for new learning" are descriptive phrases that typify the responses of the employees in sex-atypical positions, even in the two least satisfying jobs.

Perhaps the stress of the sex-atypical positions combined with attraction to the work itself may have led to the greater work satisfaction that the New Types experienced. As they have reported, they have experienced great pressure to do their jobs well, early in their work experience and later on as well. This pressure may have stimulated the kind of involvement that breeds commitment. As Locke points out, challenge heightens involvement with work; coping successfully with challenge enhances commitment to work.[7] Perhaps it was the pressure to do the job especially well that created a condition in which "actions and outcomes for which one takes personal responsibility will ordinarily produce greater effect than those for which one is not responsible, because more of oneself (i.e., one's ego) is involved in the job."[8] Although we will discuss the extra pressure phenomenon later and attempt to understand its origins, it is appropriate now to suggest that the extra pressure experienced by the occupants of sex-atypical positions may have energized the commitment to work itself—a commitment that leads to greater work satisfaction.

Stress, Counterstress

Despite the frequent report of discomfort for the men and women who occupied sex-atypical positions, their work-related affect is more positive than their peers in the least satisfying jobs. Perhaps the stress condition created by occupancy of a sex-atypical position in an unsatisfying work situation acted as positive stimulation.

Perhaps the discomfort created by occupancy of a sex-atypical position fulfills the definition of challenge, which has been identified by some as a neglected part of stress theory and research[9] as well as a central part of theory and research about work satisfaction.[10] Until now we have considered stress a negative phenomenon and generally predicted negative consequences in its wake. Such value-laden predictions, that stress is inherently harmful, bias the directions of research and possibilities for alternative understandings of such phenomena.

This study offers evidence to further counteract negative predictions and to confirm Selye's contention that positive or therapeutic value results when different forms of stress are introduced into a disabling situation, especially if the disability is chronic.[11] Selye's references emphasize adaptations to physical disease, but such logic may be applied to the interpretation of the regression analysis results for this work situation. Perhaps the least satisfying jobs are parallel to situations in which "during chronic exposure to certain irritants, our adaptive mechanisms would 'get into a groove' and stress would help us to snap out of it."[12]

Further Questions

While these results and discussion have been provocative, many questions are left unanswered. So far these analyses pertain only to those who have remained in their jobs. We sought no information about individual traits or needs for the sample group and can thus make no statement about personal differences that determined or influenced a move into a sex-atypical position.

Clearly work satisfaction is neither the most salient consequence of stress conditions nor the single most important focus of this study. Still, in many ways work satisfaction, especially as measured on the JDI, serves as a substitute measure that addresses at least some of the complex issues attached to the question of individual responses to an organizational situation. Because more than one outcome measure is important to understanding responses to any work situation, I carried out a series of regression analyses on other important outcome variables, the most important being absenteeism. Other variables and their analyses are presented and discussed in appendix E.

Absences

One response to stress that has implications for both individuals and organization is withdrawal, which manifests itself as absenteeism. Absences are behavioral evidence of a response to stress, whether that response is direct withdrawal from the work place or the more indirect result of illness or disability. Absences are important to social epidemiologists as well as to management, whose productivity goals are jeopardized by high rates of absence among employees.

In this regression analysis of absences, the same organizational, situational, and personal variables were combined in the full model equation. These twenty variables accounted for an R^2 of 0.33 and an $\bar{R}^2$ of 0.16. Following the backward elimination procedure, the final equation included five variables, which accounted for an R^2 of 0.24 and an $\bar{R}^2$ of 0.20. Variables included in the final equation are listed in table 4.

The b values and the comparative information they provide show that the longer one has been in one's job, the fewer absences one will report. New Types report fewer absences than Same Type employees in general. Those in the clerical-service job are likely to report more absences than those in other jobs, although those in the junior crafts job report far more absences than any other job group. Sex-atypical occupancy of the junior craft job (females) alleviates the rate of absence somewhat, although the overwhelming determinant of absenteeism remains occupancy of the junior crafts job. If we did not know that a person occupied the junior craft job, we would lose most of what we know about conditions that foster absences for this employee group. Again the junior crafts job is implicated as a potent stressor in its determination of absences. For this analysis, unlike the analysis of work satisfaction, the alleviating func-

Table 4
Absences: Final Model

	b	s.e.(b)	Beta	F	Usefulness
Length of Time in Job	−0.019	0.013	−0.179	2.53	0.02
Sex-Typical/ Sex-Atypical Position	−0.926	0.472	−0.199	3.84	0.02
Clerical-Service Job	1.01	0.496	0.212	4.16	0.02
Junior Craft Job	3.28	0.633	0.59	26.76	0.21
Sex-Atypicals in Junior Craft Job	1.65	1.13	0.139	2.11	0.02

Constant 2.54

tion of sex-atypical job occupancy in this job is a less potent, though discernible influence on absences.

Discussion: Organizational Characteristics and Personal Outcomes

The original questions on which this study was based anticipated differences between New Type and Same Type employees on identified affective, perceptual, and behavioral responses to stress. As my understanding of the organization developed, I accrued more information about a complex and changing work organization. Because of this complexity and change, I found that the original questions were inadequate representations of organizational reality and required amplification through new evidence and analytic techniques. The addition of regression analysis on a group of selected variables clarified my understanding of the organization, specified points of difficulty, and contributed theoretical suggestions about stress-related research.

A full range of regression analyses (appendix D) on the dependent variables revealed certain themes. Occupancy of the junior craft job is most dramatic as an influence on work satisfaction, absenteeism, self-perceived appropriateness of the job, and social support from the boss. For work satisfaction, self-perceived appropriateness of the job, and to a lesser extent absences, regression analysis revealed that sex-atypical occupancy of the junior crafts job exerts a positive countereffect, a finding that supports Selye's hypotheses about the effect of counterstress in a chronically disabling situation.

The analyses offer still more data about work experiences of female occupants of the junior crafts job. These women, while reporting more work satisfaction than their peers and slightly fewer absences than their peers (though more than others in the sample), are at the same time reporting more depression and less optimism about potential future movement. This correspondence makes sense if we appreciate the vulnerable position of the females in the junior craft job; they will be among the first released when cutbacks are introduced (they do not have seniority in these positions). Loss of these positions usually means a demotion to some form of menial work, although other limited choices are available. Women in this position may feel helpless, a feeling that could result from the threat of losing a valuable, satisfying job and that could, in turn, lead to depression. It is not inconsistent for work satisfaction to coexist with withdrawal through absence, depression, and pessimism about future organizational mobility. In fact, work satisfaction may make the potential loss of a job all the more disappointing and distressing.

Summary

Building from the initial comparisons between sex-typical and sex-atypical employees, I found that predictions of negative work-related affect, self-percept, and behavior for New Types were not confirmed in these analyses. Instead, a far more complex picture of the intersecting effects of organizational reality has emerged. Both empirical and theoretical implications come to the fore. Empirically it is apparent that certain work situations are less satisfying than others and that in those situations, New Types are less affected by dissatisfaction than Same Types. The theoretical implications of this evidence pertain to Selye's hypotheses about the mitigating effect of a second stress condition in a chronic stress situation. Similarly a theoretical connection between a stress condition and work satisfaction has been proposed; the intervening theoretical link is identified as the pressure and consequent commitment felt by the sex-atypical employees. The larger implications of this finding pertain to the generally negative expectations about the disabling effects of stress. Perhaps ability rather than disability follows certain stress conditions.

Clearly more has been learned empirically and theoretically from the application of complex multivariate analysis than from the original sets of comparisons between two groups. Still the more sophisticated analyses would not have been as effective if the awareness of organizational reality had not been included as data in the study. Without knowledge about the conditions of each job in the sample, the refined distinctions that yielded the most salient results would not have been possible. The most sophisticated multivariate techniques could not have created the information acquired by immersion in the organization. On the other hand, without appropriate analytic techniques, such information would have been only local color and not the source of important future directions for research, theory, and organizational practice.

Q:
If you had the chance to move into a woman's job, what kinds of questions would you have about it?

A:
I wouldn't want it to be totally feminine work. What kind of people would I work with? Is it a dead-end job? Like the company nurse job—that's only been done by women—I wouldn't want that. I wouldn't want to work with all women. Are they the same social class? Do we have anything in common?

A:
Would I feel comfortable doing it? Just the idea of being in a women's job makes me uncomfortable. I wouldn't like the comments of my peers, the other guys. The major part is that I personally would feel less masculine.

A:
What does the job entail? Is it dealing with women all the time? Women are so temperamental to work with. They are up one day and down the other. It's very hard to work with women.

A:
I've worked with women before and it's rotten. I don't want to but I'm a realist. Any dirty jobs to do the man has to do it. Then the women say they're doing the same job but they're not.

A:
I'd wonder about the atmosphere. I'd be concerned if it was all women. The atmosphere would be quieter. No swearing, hollering at each other. It wouldn't be as relaxed. Besides perfume is too much for me.

Q:
If you had the chance to move into a man's job, what kinds of questions would you have about it?

A:
If I had to work closely with a group of men, I'd worry about their acceptance of me. I'd want to pull my own weight. Nine out of 10 times you'd probably have to prove yourself to your co-workers. Men can't accept that women can do the job as well as they do.

A:
I'd feel odd being the only woman. I'd worry about being ostracized. I'd feel pressure to do a better job than anyone else. That happens more for women in a man's job. People expect women to prove themselves more than men. No one here expects men in this job to be superfantastic. People don't expect men to be good at clerical work. If his work isn't neat, then it's because he's a man. More excuses are made for a man.

A:
My husband wouldn't like me doing it. I'd feel uneasy working with a bunch of guys and being the only woman. I'd stick out like a sore thumb; but they'd probably behave like gentlemen. Still, I'd be lonely. I wonder how my husband would feel—probably jealous.

A:
I'd be unsure that I'd meet up with their standards—what they would expect of me. I'd want to pull my own weight. I need to be as good, if not better than men.

A:
Men are different from women. They think a girl should be home having kids. I think they're partly right. Any woman who takes a man's job would have to prove herself because girls don't belong there. That's not true for a man in a girl's job. They don't need to prove themselves. They should be as good as a girl in that job.

Anticipation

Listen carefully to the words of men and women who answered a question about changing their jobs. On the surface the question itself is quite simple and straightforward, but the responses hint at complex attitudes and feelings about men, women, and work. As individual expressions, these words are the voices of unique people; they are personal and perhaps idiosyncratic. Still the themes they suggest refer to a more universal contemporary social reality. Recent social patterns have encouraged changes in job occupancy for men and women. The meaning of these changes for individuals portends meaning for group and organizational life.

No matter how sophisticated the analyses, how much variation is explained, statistics and formulas portray only a silhouette of any situation. "Local color" becomes a necessity, not a luxury, since it fills in the blanks left by aggregate data and numbers. From personal words and descriptions emerge attitudes and feelings and another sense of meaning.

In beginning this chapter, I contrasted the words of men and women Same Types in response to a question about sex-atypical job occupancy. Their words imply far more than is actually stated; they reveal the complexity of the speaker's feelings in response to a "suppose" question. The women talk about their concerns about being adequate for the job, about their acceptance by men, about being excluded, about husbands' jealousy, about their own conflicts about where they "belong" (home with the kids?). The men speak about what it would mean about their masculinity, their careers, their differences with those already in the job, their dislike of women.

These words are echoed throughout the following chapters. Some of the concerns are different from the worries and experiences of men and women who took New Type jobs; some of the concerns reflect

what was actually felt and what actually occurred for
many. But there seems to be some convergence between the attitudes and expectations of those who did not make the moves and those who did.

To explore in more depth the words, meanings, and reflected experiences of the people who participated in this work, I have organized the next two chapters around a chronological framework. Beginning with the anticipation of those who did not make the moves about the potential of making such moves, I then turn to the actual patterns of those New Types who did make these moves and to corollary reports from Same Types who were in work groups entered by a New Type man or woman.[1]

As background for these reports, the length of time in the job for the New Type employees is presented in table 5. Women New Types had been in their jobs longer at the time of the interviews.

Taking the Job

In conversations with men and women who had taken the New Type positions, we asked their reasons for taking the positions and their feelings or apprehensions before moving into these positions. There were

Table 5
Time in Job for New Type Employees

Females	Males	Years
3	9	less than 1
7	12	1–2
8	2	3
5	1	4
2	1	Over 4

differences between males and females on both questions that reflected, in part, thematic differences evident in the larger sample of men and women. The New Type men most often took their jobs as stepping-stones and focused on this aspect when questioned.

I don't particularly like the traditional male jobs. This is stimulating work for me. Besides there is always the prestige of an office job, which is good if you want to move up in a company.

It used to be a macho thing that men worked physically. Now you establish goals and see how to get there. Promotional opportunities are available in this job; they aren't in some of the others.

I wouldn't have taken this position unless I had a goal to reach within the company beyond this position. The question is where can I go from here?

To better myself in experience—to give myself a base for promotion. I don't think it's a man's job.

I can perform better than a girl in it. It's a training base for lower-level management for a man, who has a better opportunity than a woman who wants to be a supervisor.

I took it for the promotional opportunities. I also enjoy mental work—seeing a complex job through to completion.

When asked whether they had questions and apprehensions about taking a job typically done by women, these men often said that they had no worries about moving into the job. One man, in a representative response, commented:

None. I didn't feel it was degrading me; didn't think I was being feminine. It was more money.

Another man:

I didn't really have any [questions or apprehensions]. There were no doubts that I would have any problems working with women.

And another:

I thought it might be easier for opposites to get along than for women.

Among those who admitted that they did have questions or apprehensions, the male focus was on "getting along" or "fitting in" with women.

Will I get along with women? I've heard from friends that working with women is hard. You have to put up with comments about why a man would want a woman's job.

I wondered about what it would be like to break the ice.

I was worried about how the women would react to me.

Would I work for a woman? The outlook of a female supervisor is different. She seems to think she has to prove she can do a man's job.

The women in New Type positions more vividly recalled question and apprehension than did the men.[2] Still the women's responses to this question varied. Those who had been exposed to the new position through previous clerical work related to their present job had the fewest apprehensions about taking the job. As one woman noted:

I had no questions, not after those years as a clerk. I'd had a lot of exposure to it. Just because it's traditionally been a man's job doesn't mean it has to be a man's job. Anybody can do it. They've been bluffing all along. It doesn't take much to do this job.

Many of the other females in New Type positions had questions about taking their jobs in the first place. These questions were of two types: about acceptance and about ability. About acceptance:

I did worry about being accepted by the men.

Would I be accepted or would I have a hard time? I worried that men would think I should be home cooking and cleaning.

I worried about whether they would like me. I wondered about how the fellows would feel about a girl coming into the group.

About ability:

> Because I didn't know what it entailed; I had no background in it. Before I took it I wondered whether I could do it.

> I thought I would never learn it and that the men wouldn't want me on it.

A third cluster of responses came from some women who had moved into these positions. These women did not have previous exposure to the jobs, but in response to questions about apprehensions, they emphasized the rewards of the jobs (pay and desirable work) or the challenge of the situation. These women spoke of their enjoyment of challenges and risk. As one woman commented:

> There are a lot of people here who think that women should do clerical jobs. I like to work with my hands though. I figured I'd give it my best shot and if it didn't turn out, ok.

No simple generalizations can encompass all the New Type males' or females' prejob apprehensions. There is a difference between the two groups in the range of questions mentioned. The men mentioned fewer questions and a more limited range of concern than the women. Women who had the fewest apprehensions or questions about their sex-atypical positions were those who knew more about what the positions entailed, based on their exposure to the jobs. Those with the most apprehensions had had the least information about the jobs. The concerns of the women in general clustered around questions of acceptance and ability. Will the men accept me? Can I do the job? Questions about ability to do the job were less important to those with most information about the jobs, since they did know more about the match of their abilities with the requirements of the job. For those with less information, mystery about job requirements seemed to contribute to apprehension about ability.

Many of the women—no matter what their ap-

prehensions about ability or acceptance—mentioned
the challenge inherent in the situation. "It's a challenge. A woman has as much right to use her mind
and intelligence as a man."

Before the Job: The Host Group

When appropriate, we asked the sex-typical employees to describe the work climate before the arrival
of the first New Type and to share some of the questions and apprehensions discussed by the Same
Types before the entry.

The men in sex-typical positions before the arrival
of the first New Type women remembered asking or
thinking about questions such as these:

What work would she be doing? Was she good looking?

We hoped that she was good looking.

We were worried—can we swear? Why would she want a
job where she's the only woman?

We didn't think it was right to get a big jump into this job.
She shouldn't be taking a man's job.

Was she capable? Would she pull her share of the load?

We were apprehensive. Could she do the job?

There was a negative attitude in general toward the woman.
We wondered about her background. How much would she
know? Could she do the job?

We'd have to watch what we said. Can she do the job? How
does she look?

Some thought they [women] could handle it. Some were
bitter. There were jokes about them. Some guys would tell
them, Go home to the kitchen—and they meant it. Others
were friendly.

All these men reported jokes about the woman before
her arrival, but only one was willing to share examples of these jokes.

The conversations reported by women in sex-typical positions paralleled those of the males in some respects and differed in others. A few of the women mentioned questions about the man's ability to handle the job.

We didn't think a man could hack it; wouldn't have the patience or tolerance; couldn't do filing; wouldn't be as involved as a woman. He couldn't do *our* job.

Other concerns were about changes in the work climate.

We were worried that we'd have to watch our language like about general girl things and personal things, like about your period. We worried about whether we could be ourselves.

Numerous comments pertained to sexuality. Some of the women reported interest in the male's attractiveness, similar to the male's report.

The single girls were dying to see what they [the new males] looked like.

Still the preponderance of the comments from the women, unlike those of the men, were questions about why a man would want this woman's job. Was he "funny"? Was he "queer"?

We wondered why he was taking *this* job. When we saw him, we said, He's not bad. Then we *really* wondered why he was coming to this job.

We wondered if the guy was straight. Why would he want a job like this?

We imagined the kind of guy who would want this job. Would he be gay?

We kidded about his having to wear a skirt.

We wondered, What does he look like? Is he strange? Does he wear earrings? No one actually asked if he was straight or gay, since it was some time ago and you didn't talk about things like that. But I think that was behind the jokes about the earrings.

These women reported that jokes before the first

man's arrival generally referred to clothing, hair style, jewelry—attributions about effeminacy. According to one person, these discussions evoked much giggling.

The Host Setting: Differences and Similarities

The arrival of the sex-atypical males and females certainly created some stir. For the men, the stir seemed to emerge in the form of questions about changes in the work climate, the woman's attractiveness, and her ability to do the job. There was some question about why she would want a man's job, but this was limited, since it was generally agreed that women would want the better pay attached to a man's job. There was also some expression of bitterness about the replacement of a male by a female, but this expression also seemed to be limited in scope. Apparently the men did share jokes in anticipation of the women's arrival, but we could get little information about the content of them. The men's question about the women's ability to do the job echoed some of the concerns of the New Type women before their moves into the job.

For the women, the stir about the arrival of men generated concerns parallel to and divergent from the concerns of their male counterparts. They worried about changes in the work climate, just as the men had. "Will we be able to be ourselves?" There was far less mention of the males' ability to do the female-typed job; only one respondent expounded on this point. There was some emphasis on the attractiveness of the incoming man, very similar to the anticipations of some of the male Same Types.

The striking difference between the male and female host groups came from the females' questions, Why would a man want a woman's job? What is the matter with him? The attribution of motive to the men who had moved into these positions was frequent. After promotion, the motive most frequently attributed to this "deviant" job choice was deviance in sexuality. The general message from these women, before knowing the men, was that something has to be wrong with a guy who wants a woman's job.

Starting Out in the Job

Into these different kinds of work setting came men and women with different concerns about their place in the setting. What happened to them when they arrived is the next focus of interest. We asked parallel questions of newcomers and host group members to describe the behavior and communication in these settings during newcomers' early time on the job. These reports are important to understanding the potential difficulties of movement into these positions, and they have both theoretical and practical implications. For anchor points to questions about initial behavior toward the New Type by the host group peers and supervisor, we relied on the initial findings of Meyer and Lee[3] in their study of women in sex-atypical positions in public utilities. Meyer and Lee categorized host behavior as accepting, neutral, or rejecting. Along these dimensions we asked about the behavior of peers and supervisors toward the New Type newcomer at entry.

Supervisor's Welcome

The Same Type men and women were asked about the initial behavior of their supervisors when they first came to the job. In addition to questions about acceptance, neutrality, or rejection, we asked about the supervisor's attention, helpfulness, difference in treatment. For all these questions, most respondents answered positively, so there was no significant difference between the men and women in their description of supervisor's behaviors.

On the other hand, when male and female members of the host groups were asked to describe supervisory behavior toward the New Type employees, their reports were somewhat more differentiated. There was a significant difference between males and females, although the difference was more of degree than of kind. When asked to describe supervisory behavior to the newcomers, Same Type men and women responded as shown in table 6.

Same Type males describe less accepting and more rejecting supervisory behavior toward New Type females than that described by Same Type female employees about their supervisors. Still, when pressed for descriptive details about those behaviors, few were reported.

He wasn't too keen on the idea of having women here. He expected her not to do well.

Supervisors were accepting only because they had to be accepting.

He kept a closer eye on her.

Since none of the female respondents reported rejecting behavior from supervisors to the new men, we have no comparable examples. Of the very accepting supervisory behavior reported by host group females, the most frequently mentioned were tolerance of error by the new male workers and at times more attention and help than was normally provided to the incoming female worker. Some of the women expressed resentment that the new male employees were treated more leniently and that supervisors made fewer demands on them. On the other hand,

Table 6
Same Types' Views of Supervisory Behavior toward New Type

	Female	Male
Very Rejecting	0	1
Rejecting	0	2
Neutral	1	3
Accepting	6	16
Very Accepting	17	1
	24	23

some women reported that the men received more critical attention than usual.

Peer Welcome

The men and women New Types differed little in their descriptions of the behavior of new work peers toward them. When asked whether peers were accepting, neutral, or rejecting when they first took the job, most (83 percent) answered *somewhat accepting* and qualified that with references to the "one or two" people who had been particularly difficult at first or with references to being excluded from conversations. The women referred more to the "one or two" difficult individuals, while the men more often considered exclusions from general conversations the most detracting feature of their entry.[4]

Some of the women New Types described their early reception by peers in terms quite different from those of their peers, while others paralleled the male report of helpfulness and interest.

Some tried to make it really rotten. They were trying to gross me out by talking really dirty. When I told them not to, they kept right on.

One guy gave me a hard time. He didn't like women. The others made him shut up.

They sometimes went overboard to help me out when I didn't want it.

There was a good group. They didn't want to be called male chauvinist, so they eased up on teasing and stunts after a month.

The guys did treat me differently—they wanted to do everything for me.

They couldn't do enough to explain things to me. They knew I didn't have the background—drew it all out for me. It was fantastic.

There was no resentment here that I could feel or see. Most came later when some women were promoted to a more advanced job.

When the male Same Types were asked about their
reception of women in New Type jobs, they were
more likely to report neutral, rejecting, or very rejecting behavior than were Same Type women about
their reception of New Type men. Still, the reports of
the New Type females corresponded with those of
their Same Type male peers; more than half the male
group reported that females were accepted when they
began their jobs, as indicated in table 7. Table 7 also
indicates that Same Type males reported more rejecting peer behavior toward the New Type females than
did Same Type females toward New Type males.

In describing peer behavior and attitudes to female
newcomers, male Same Types observed a spectrum
of responses.

Lots of guys resented her being here—and didn't want to
show her things. She was the first woman and we didn't
know how many more would be coming. Some of them had
more seniority and we wondered if they would take our
jobs.

People weren't too ready to help her to explain things. They
gave her the cold shoulder.

The guys were overly accepting of a woman. *I* had to learn
the job on my own. People bent over backwards to help *her.*

We treated her as the weaker sex, but then we accepted her
as she proved she could do the job.

We tried to be extra helpful—to help the underdog.

Table 7
Same Types' Views of Peer Behavior toward New Type
Newcomers

	Female	Male
Very Rejecting	0	2
Rejecting	0	5
Neutral	0	2
Accepting	8	10
Very Accepting	16	4
	24	23

We didn't expect as good output from a woman so we probably watched closer.

I am rejecting to females on this job and have been from the start.

I think the approach is different. There is more lenience given to females. Nobody jumps down a woman's throat if she makes a mistake like they do to a guy.

The host group women also reported a variety of responses to incoming males.

We're pretty helpful in this office to a new person no matter who it is.

We kind of spoiled the first few, since they were different. We felt sorry for the poor guys.

Since he was a man we all tried to help him out. It *is* easier for a woman to do clerical work.

We gave the guy more positive attention probably because a woman has a sense of direction in this job and a man just doesn't have it.

We were more protective of the guys at first.

They overdid it. Sometimes they even did some of his work for him. The other women were much more helpful to him and paid more attention to him.

We realized it wasn't his fault that he was here. They just offered it to him and he took it. So we tried to be nice to him.

In general, the females reported more kindness to men than males did to women. Perhaps because females had begun to make their transitions earlier than the men—during a period of less enlightened social and organizational attitudes or before such transitions became accepted as fact—their entry was more difficult than the more recent entry of males into all-female settings. For these reasons and others the females may have been received less favorably by their peers than were the males. But even for the women New Types the extra attention was some-

times intended to be positive, despite the more frequently reported negative experiences.

Teasing

The male and females in sex-atypical positions reported significant differences in teasing from peers
when they first took their jobs; females reported re-
ceiving much more teasing than men in New Type
jobs, as indicated in table 8.

The males in the host group agreed with the female
New Types and reported more often that women
were teased, as indicated in table 9. Thus the two
groups agree that women received more teasing from
men when they first entered their jobs.

When asked to describe some of the teasing they
experienced, a few women became voluble with
anecdotes, some of which evoked laughter and some
of which still evoked pained expressions. Many
women reported remarks that were made (and still
are made) when they asked a question or made a
mistake ("It's just like a woman") or when a mistake
was picked up ("One of the girls must have done it").

Table 8
Teasing: New Types "Getting It"

	Female	Male
No Teasing	8	19
Some Teasing	8	3
Much Teasing	9	3
	25	25

Table 9
Teasing: Same Types "Dishing it Out"

	Female	Male
No Teasing	10	3
Some Teasing	1	8
Much Teasing	5	5
	16	16

These remarks were communicated as put-downs and experienced as insults by the women who reported their frequency.

Such remarks form a subsample of the teasing recalled by women. Many remarks referred to women's job competence.

They picked on me by criticizing my work and style.

It bothers you when they pick on little things.

They were critical of my work and the way I did it. That really made me nervous in the beginning.

A secondary topic for teasing was the woman's physical "fit" with the job. From two women in the same job, I heard two comments.

They teased me about my size and said I was too small to do the job.

They teased me about being too tall. They said I was clumsy.

The personal remarks about competence, mistakes, and fit with the job seemed to evoke the most distress among the newcomers. They all reported that over time they developed some interpersonal coping mechanism for responding to the teasing and noted that their distress decreased over time. But attacks on competence seemed to continue, and to continue to bother these women.

Teasing was most common in the crafts jobs. Women had entered the crafts jobs earlier, and most craft employees were generally younger, two conditions which seemed more conducive to teasing. Often women reported that they were "tested" with foul language and dirty jokes, most of which subsided after they had ignored the provocation or laughed along with the rest of the group. One woman recalled hilarity around the appearance of realistic plastic spiders and insects in her lunch but hastened to point out that this behavior has since been directed toward male newcomers as well. A few women were asked if they had come to do the cleaning or dusting. These remarks were bothersome, but the women generally shrugged them off.

For the 24 percent of the New Type men who reported being teased by the host women, their examples took different forms. Two men, new to their jobs, observed that the females in the host setting resented men moving in and were fearful that the men would move up in the organization. In these situations, according to the New Type males, women were particularly alert to the errors made by the new male workers and pointed them out to the men and to the supervisors. One man reported that he had been sent a half-eaten sandwich in the mail and that the plug on his typewriter was pulled out, both kinds of behavior he enjoyed ("I ride with the punches").

A few of the men were also teased about the way they did their work. One man noted that he learned aspects of the job, such as filing, quite slowly and that his pace earned him the nickname "Speedy." Another said that he was teased about his handwriting but observed, "I enjoyed it. Teasing makes you feel accepted."

Teasing: Meaning and Consequences

For most of the respondents, teasing did not mean acceptance, it meant a kind of testing that seemed to diminish with time. Much of the banter, foul language, and dirty jokes seemed to become less intense over time, although it is hard to know whether the respondents became less sensitive or whether there was in fact less to provoke reaction. In general, the only kind of teasing that persisted and was troublesome was the put-down of women's competence, both individually and as a group. Although most women reported that they shrugged off these remarks after a while, there was often a note of continuing sensitivity.

One consequence of this sensitivity *may* be evident in the responses of New Type males and females to a question about fitting in on the job: Did it take you any longer than other employees to feel that you fit in here? As table 10 shows, there are differences between the males and females in sex-atypical positions in their comparative assessments of fitting in. More of the New Type females thought that it took them longer than their male peers to fit in, while an equal number of New Type males reported that it took them a shorter time to fit in, an assessment made by none of the New Type women.

Doing the Job: Extra Pressure

I have mentioned the dramatic difference ($f = 114.5$, $p < 0.000$) between the New Type and Same Type employees in their responses to the question, When you first started work here, did you feel extra pressure to do the job especially well? There was no significant difference between the male and female New Types in the frequency with which they responded *always* to this question. There were also similarities in the type of language used to discuss the extra pressure. They often used the words "challenge," "proving," or "defeat" in their explanations of this feeling. When asked where this pressure came from, self or others, most men and women said it came from themselves, that they applied standards to themselves in all work situations or in everything they did. The few who mentioned others as a source of pressure also mentioned

Table 10
New Types' Time to "Fit In"

	Female	Male
Shorter	0	10
Same	15	8
Longer	10	7
	25	25

teasing and criticism from peers as a source of self-consciousness or of excessive supervisory attention to error as a stimulus for pressure to do the job well.

Despite the similarities between the men and women in their reported experience of extra pressure, there is some difference between them in their explanation about the experience, though that difference is subtle and not readily apparent. When men's and women's verbatim explanations of this experience are compared, themes specific to men and to women emerge from the verbatim statements.

Men

I didn't want to be treated like a woman on the job. I'm not as emotional as some of the girls, and I wanted people to notice that.

I felt extra pressure. People expected me to do the job well. Thought I was the only one here who had gone to college. Felt I should pick things up quicker than the girls.

I wanted to show people that a man can do the job.

I like to be on top. I gave it all I had to be on top. There was no outside pressure.

I was concerned with getting everything right and in on time. They told me not to worry, but it didn't matter. If I had been a failure, there would have been some ego factor. Why can't I do it if a woman can?

I always feel extra pressure in the work I do, especially when I'm thinking about a promotion, which I am now.

Being in a minority here, people were watching me more than others. After three months, I asked how I was doing, and my supervisor said fine; but I still didn't feel less pressure.

I always feel extra pressures, especially when I'm working with people who are threatened by me.

Women

I worried that I'd never learn the job and that the men wouldn't want me in it.

I felt I had to do the best I can. I'll show that just because I'm a woman doesn't mean I can't do the job.

Because I'm trying to show that picking me wasn't a mistake.

I wanted to prove that I could do it and comprehend what they were teaching me. They would say "It's just like a woman" and that I couldn't handle it if I didn't stay.

You feel inferior about your abilities to begin with, and that teasing gets you thinking and you get mad. You keep it inside; you don't give it back to the guys. . . . I'm still not really sure how good I am at this job.

I wanted to prove myself. You're new to a job that has been held by men. Comments have been made by men about women saying we couldn't do it, couldn't make it in the job.

I'm going to do extra well because I'm not going to let those guys beat me out.

Different themes characterize these responses. The men spoke frequently about a need to do the job so well that they would be viewed differently from the women. Thus they worked especially hard. One man felt he was expected to do the job well because he had better credentials than others (college education). The men in general felt the pressure because they were supposed to do better. To be unable to do a job that could be done (even) by a woman would be a blow to their egos.

The women, on the other hand, expressed worry about lack of ability to do the job and exclusion by the men because of their incompetence. Women felt underequipped for the job. Thus the pressure to perform was impelled by a double negative—the need to show that one was not inadequate. Their comments reveal the feelings of inferiority and incapability that they frequently expressed as a source of their concerns. Many woman attributed their drive to "prove" themselves to these feelings. Whatever the reasons given by men and women, the feeling of extra pressure for performance was shared by the New Types.

It would have been intriguing to present the question about extra pressure to New Type men and women who did not remain in their jobs to compare the responses of those who "made it" and those who left. Although such direct comparisons combined with a longitudinal perspective would have been optimal, the research situation did not permit them.

A fortuitous combination of information sources provided another perspective on potentially comparative experiences and offered some insight into the individual experiences of New Type men and women who had not stayed in these jobs. Personal testimony from some of these people combined with some turnover data has added some information about the situation for these people.

Coincidentally, two of the females in our sample had previously occupied sex-atypical positions. One was presently in a sex-typical clerical position, and the other presently occupied a sex-atypical crafts job. Additional and slightly different information is provided by company-initiated interviews of men who did not complete the training program for one of the clerical positions; this study was undertaken to diagnose difficulties that were discouraging to male entrants. More detail is added by our interview with a male clerical employee who had requested a medical transfer from his job because of his inability to do the work. These media offer glimpses of a work experience that seems to differ from others in the study.

Of the two women who had left previous sex-atypical positions, one left because of her inability to "make it," according to her report, and the other was removed in an overall cutback of one of the male crafts positions. Losing a position as the result of a general cutback is a different personal experience from losing a position because of personal inability, and the two respondents reflected this difference. The job held by the woman who had been removed by cutback had been one of the most visibly "male" jobs in the organization, one which required physical agility and willingness to tolerate physical discomfort. This woman had been one of few females in the job, all of whose positions were cut back. She reported that her experience in this job was extremely positive. Her experience was enhanced and supported by the presence of another woman in her work group who was learning the job at the same time as well as by male peers and supervisors who were helpful, friendly, and supportive of the women.

There were a lot of warm feelings among us. We got to be like a couple of mascots. It was like having a bunch of brothers.

Despite acceptance by both peers and supervisor, the two women found the job difficult, found winter outdoor work frightening and dangerous, and could often be found "crying together in the bathroom where no one could see us." The difficulties she expressed were related to the nature of the task rather than to the work climate, and she believed that over time she would have found the task less difficult. Unfortunately the economy did not let time work in her behalf. Her next job was in janitorial work, followed by her current clerical position. From her point of view, the most compelling stress condition in her experience was movement into a janitorial position, which she and other women attempted to contest as a women's rights issue to no avail. She reported:

When we were canned we tried to do something through the women's rights office. As long as there's a cutback, Affirmative Action gets thrown out the window. It's a beautiful way for the company to get rid of us legally. I got thrown into a really terrible position.

Another woman who was randomly included in the sample as a member of the junior crafts job category reported in the interview that she had had a brief experience in the senior crafts position. Before begin-

ning that position, she had been the first woman in
the junior crafts job in her area, so she had been
through the experience of being the first woman in a
previously male job. She felt that a number of factors
were operating against her success when she was
asked to move into the senior crafts job, although she
was not aware of them at the time. She felt that she
was picked for the position only "because they
wanted a girl." She was placed in a self-paced learning situation for the job, while a man who was
selected at the time went into a class with other
people, an arrangement that she would have pre-
ferred. Since she had been in a car accident right
before the training, she felt especially vulnerable.

I wouldn't do it again. I was a nervous wreck. It was too
much for me. I almost landed back in the hospital. I still feel
resentment toward the guy who put me in that class; I think
he wanted to prove to me that there was a point where I
couldn't go. He knew I couldn't do that job, at least with that
kind of training; there was a lot of pressure in it. I lost my
confidence and really felt bad when I couldn't make it, but I
knew the job wasn't for me.

This woman attributes her difficulties in learning the
job to the foreman's undermining behavior, the programmed learning approach to training, and insuffi-
cient time on the previous job. When asked about
possible ways in which this experience might have
been more successful, she noted that she would have
done better in a classroom learning situation with
other students around. Although she did have quite a
bit of information about the job from her daily work
with it, she noted that if she had been more alert to
the pressures of the job, she might not have taken it
on. She blamed her boss for not having discussed this
carefully with her before she moved into the new
position.

Losses of male clerical workers in training have
recently been investigated systematically by the
company. Interviews conducted by personnel staff in

1975 revealed that a number of the men who began training for clerical positions dropped out of training early because the job was quite different from what they had anticipated. Of the five men interviewed by the company, all felt that they had not been given an accurate picture of the job and that the job presented more pressures and simultaneous demands than each had anticipated. One man commented that the training itself was "too hectic and too much, too fast" and "confusing at times," a situation for which he felt completely unprepared.

Another source of information about those who leave sex-atypical jobs comes from a participant, one of the male clerical employees who had been in his position ten months. He anticipated that he would soon be leaving his job, based on his request for a transfer on medical grounds. He disliked the job in general and found it intensely pressured and constantly frustrating. He reported that when he first began, he did have some apprehensions about taking a job about which he knew nothing but felt that since it was a stepping-stone and offered a decent wage and job security, it would work out all right. He reported that he was well treated by peers, who were generally helpful in his training, although he felt that his supervisor should have provided more time and instruction on the job. He noted that the job required a "drastic adaptation" following his previous job as an office messenger. Despite reports about the general helpfulness of his female co-workers, he did report feeling left out at lunch times, when the women went together to the women's lounge and left him alone in another lounge. He did request that another man go to lunch at the same time so that it wouldn't be so lonely. He felt, essentially, that he hadn't "made it" in the job.

That's a very disappointing feeling, to know that you're not able to do what you still believe you can do. I have to say it must be me. I can't blame anyone else.

From our interview it is hard to understand what differentiated this man's experience from those who moved more effectively into the job at the same time, in the same office. He did report that he was a very "sensitive" person.

Although each of these situations differs in its superficial characteristics, they share some common features. All those who didn't "make it" in training or in the early period of the job reported being unprepared for the kinds of pressure in that particular job or training situation. In some circumstances they felt unsupported in an attempt to manage them. There were no claims of overt discrimination because of sex, although there was some complaint of supervisory inattention at times as well as concern about trainer and supervisor impatience with their learning pace.

The company has made some attempt to counteract the difficulties reported by these "dropouts," especially from the largest clerical category. Turnover rates show that the number of males leaving this position and moving down or out of the organization remains a problem, though proportionally a smaller problem than in previous years.

Company statistics about turnover are revealing, although they do not clearly indicate what proportions of the New Types in each of these positions have left to return to a previous position, a move that would be an indication of not "making it" in the job during the six-month probationary period. But company records make it possible to compare the numbers of employees who move down or out of a job with the number who move up in the organization for any given year. The figures themselves do not assert that those who move down or out are not "making it." They may have been victims of comprehensive cutbacks; they may have found a better job outside the company; they may have decided to go into business for themselves. Still the patterns themselves are informative. If certain jobs seem to be characterized by

more movement out and down than up, then questions can be posed about the jobs and the turnover
rates. Although the personnel records provide no
specific information about why people left their jobs,
there should be some comparability in the personnel
recording systems.

Appendix F presents the complete spectrum of data
reflecting the overall patterns of movement out of
jobs for the four central groups of employees for the
years 1974, 1975, and 1976. Table 11 in turn, sum-
marizes this data in terms of the percentages of
moves up and down in the organization (or out).
Clearly the trends for men in sex-atypical positions
have improved somewhat between 1974 and 1976. In
1974 none of the male New Types were promoted,
and 100 percent of the men who left sex-atypical jobs

Table 11
Proportion of Movements Out of Job, 1974–1976

Group Out (%)	Moved Up (%)	Moved Down or Out (%)
1974		
Male New Types	0	100
Male Same Types	51	23
Female Same Types	56	39
Female New Types	31	63
1975		
Male New Types	40	60
Male Same Types	26	40
Female Same Types	21	61
Female New Types	0	82
1976		
Male New Types	47	53
Male Same Types	74	14
Female Same Types	30	65
Female New Types	41	54

NOTE: Percentages do not add up to 100 percent because
some reasons for termination have not been included here.
For more complete presentation of figures, see appendix F.

moved down or out of the company. In 1975 the proportions changed to 40 percent and 60 percent, respectively. In 1976 the proportions were 47 percent and 53 percent.

The female New Types showed different patterns of movement out of their jobs. Between 1974 and 1976 there was some change in the comparative proportions of female New Types moving up or down from their jobs. In 1974, 31 percent of the female New Types who left their jobs moved up; 63 percent moved down or out. In 1975, a year for less mobility in general for all groups and especially for the male Same Types and female New Types, the female New Types made no movements up and 82 percent of their movements were either down or out. These proportions were quite different from the other three groups. Later, in 1976, more female New Types moved up than had before; 41 percent of the moves were up and 54 percent were down or out of the company.

The meaning and importance of these patterns for all groups will be reconsidered in a subsequent discussion. For this discussion the comparative movement patterns of the New Types and Same Types form the central theme. For all years except 1975, when all four groups sent more of their members out or down than up, the male Same Types have generally shown more comparative upward movement than any other group. In 1976, in fact, they were the only group to send more individuals up in the organization than down or out, a proportion unmatched in direction or size by the other groups.

Were the figures to "speak for themselves," then the more personal stories behind each job departure could be known. Without those personal stories, we are left with a picture of group trends and patterns; here the picture seems to show more New Types moving down and out of their jobs than the Same Types in each year of comparison.

Boys and Girls Together

The men and women in sex-atypical positions who stayed with their training and their jobs reported that their personal and organizational work situation improved with time. Male and female Same Types reported enjoyment of the mixed sex environment: "It's nice to have women around here. It's not as boring as it used to be" and "Now that men are here, there's more joking. I like it better."

From the New Types we heard estimates of the length of time it took for employees to "get used" to each other; these estimates ranged from six months to two years, for the earliest arrivals. Sex-atypical employees who were preceded in their work settings by others like themselves required less time for acclimation, as did the host group. This was even more characteristic of work situations in which the proportion of minority representation was higher rather than lower. The following observations came from male employees in the job where women constituted 26 percent of the job occupants, the highest in proportion of the jobs studied.

They're readily accepted now. Now that women are proving they can do it they accept them right away.

Now women are coming in at a higher level. They have proved themselves here.

Moving In: Discussion

Everett Hughes observed almost thirty years ago that one consequence of the upward mobility encouraged by American democracy would be "large numbers of people of new kinds turning up in various positions." He continued: "In the stereotyped prejudices concerning others, there is usually contained the assumption that these other people are peculiarly adapted to the particular places which they have held up to the present time; it is a corollary implication that they are not quite fit for new positions to which they may aspire."[5]

Hughes's comment applies to the experiences of
men and women who have moved into sex-atypical
positions, as this movement has been described by
the newcomer males and females and the male and
female members of the host group. Hughes's observations were based on assumptions about occupational segregation familiar to sociologists. From these
assumptions and their reflections in empirical evidence comes a recognition of the boundaries, in
terms of qualifications for membership, established
around occupational groups. For some occupations,
certification and identification as a member requires
extensive training, socialization, and preparation. For
other occupations there are fewer formal barriers to
participation, but those barriers may be impenetrable
by those who do not share salient characteristics of
the modal occupational member. Many occupations
have been identified over the years with one sex, and
the appearance of a member of the other sex stimu-
lates a question.

The advent of colleague-competitors of some new and
peculiar type or by some new route is likely to arouse
anxieties.[5]

We have learned about the anxieties caused by the
arrival of new and peculiar types, especially when
those types are newest and most peculiar and when
their route to the position is purportedly different
from that taken by others. In anticipation of the arrival
of the first male or female to enter a previously sex-
typed group, employees share much concern, expressed directly in terms of questions about group life
and about the new person and indirectly in the form
of jokes and sarcasm. Members of the host group
wonder, Can we be ourselves? Can we conduct ourselves the way we usually do? Can we talk about what
we've always talked about? For newcomers who
could share or remember their apprehensions, concerns about acceptance were common, although expressed in different terms by men and women. "Will I

be accepted?" On both sides, then, the arrival of the stranger was a change that generated special tensions for both individuals and groups.

Changes and the Individual

Among the responses to this change expressed by those who made the transitions into sex-atypical occupations or work groups, the most striking was extra pressure to do their work especially well, a pressure felt almost universally by these men and women and rarely by those in sex-typical positions. Rosabeth Kanter has attributed this extra pressure to the increased visibility of the token member coming into a work situation previously dominated by one sex or ethnic group. The token is, by definition, visibly different and differently visible from the other members of that work group. In this respect the behavior, conduct, and performance of the token male or female are singled out for special attention. This visibility generates the extra attention and the extra pressure experienced by this representative of a statistical minority.

Attention from others was acknowledged by our sample as among the reasons for their feelings of pressure. Many of them noted that these feelings "came from inside me." Although no research method could delve far enough into consciousness and the unconscious to determine the actual source of this feeling, it is notable that more of the New Types attributed the source of extra pressure to themselves. Perhaps this experience pertains to the position of the "new and peculiar types" mentioned by Hughes and to the consequent feeling of "not quite fitting" into the occupational group. To feel as if they belonged, these employees felt that they had to work harder than others to demonstrate their credibility—as much to themselves as to others—as members of the occupational group.

The employees elaborated on this theme themselves. When questioned about the extra pressure, the New Type men and women referred to "proving" themselves, to "defeat," to "challenge"—as if their presence in that work situation was contested. These responses mesh in part with Hughes's anticipation of marginality for "odd kinds of fellows."[7] The New Type could not belong to the work group for the same reasons or on the same basis by which others could claim membership (by sex) and therefore had to demonstrate another claim to membership (by proving adequacy at the task).

There is more than just a sense of not belonging in the words of the New Types. There is also a sense of conflict and contest, of a struggle waged against some kind of counterpressure. Expression of this counterpressure is subtle and heard more often in the voices of the New Types than in the direct expressions of the Same Type employees. Among the Same Type employees there were reports, especially from the men, about teasing the female job incumbents and subjecting them to tests different from those applied to other newcomers. On the other hand, there was little reported direct conflict between the host group and New Types who stayed in their jobs.

For those who left their jobs there is no direct information about their reasons for leaving, but many study participants have given us their views about the departures of New Types. For those who didn't make it in the job, the reasons were always personal and individual. Most frequently these reasons were directed to the competence of the individual. He or she couldn't do the work, couldn't follow instructions, couldn't catch on fast enough. A few of those who left, especially the women in male jobs, were described as too old; one was referred to as Grandma and was considered a misfit because of her inability to do the job and her social difference (age) from the rest of the work group. Some women left for health reasons; and some, mostly men, left because they just did not like the job. Other explanations about New Types who left their jobs were offered by those who had stayed in their positions. About men who had left the job, women reported:

He said he didn't like the job—the pressure.

There were two men. They weren't pushing as hard as they could. They made a few too many mistakes.

I knew two men; they both weren't controlled enough. One was immature. They didn't understand the importance of the job. They didn't try hard enough, didn't want to work.

Men commented about women who had had New Type jobs and had left.

It was too much of a strain on her. She couldn't keep up with the job. I'm not sure she really knew her limitations.

Some women were put in the job above me and didn't make it. I don't know why but I know that I would have made it. They wasted the opportunity.

One just couldn't absorb the information.

In none of these discussions did anyone mention the group experience of the entering employee. Nowhere was group climate, welcome, or individual comfort mentioned as a source of distress to the person who left. Explanations instead "blamed the victim." Individual inadequacy or inability to fit was viewed as the cause of defection. Despite frequent comments about the change in climate with the arrival of New Types, increased tension, and changes in behavior and conversation, none of these environmental features were presented as reasons for departure.

Explanations of defections echo New Types' explanations of success. The emphasis is on the individual and his or her mastery of the work situation, most often in terms of the task itself. They also mention the capacity "not to let things get to you"; this ability was referred to frequently by those who made it when describing their earliest experiences on the job. Lack of this ability was also mentioned as a reason for failure. Those who didn't make it often "let things get to them."

None of the employees emphasized the conflicts in the work situation stimulated by the arrival of the new employees. When there was a disturbance in the inclusion process, when the worker did not stay, the cause was attributed to the employee and never to the group situation. Yet there was much indirect evidence that the work situation was characterized by tension, friction, and static between the entering New Type employees and the host Same Type group.

To state an absolute case for the presence of such tension and static, we need more long-term information about group "climate" and more understanding of the expressions of group tension and how these can be measured systematically. Still the descriptions reported by these employees suggest that a disruption did occur with new arrivals. The transposition of a man or woman into an occupation previously dominated by the other sex resulted in change.

As a source of friction and irritation for the work group and a source of tension and discomfort for the incoming individuals, the position of the New Type newcomer requires some understanding of the similarities and differences in personal and group experiences between men and women. One theoretical resource that is evolving in its sophistication and explanatory capability is intergroup theory. Intergroup theory refers to a theoretical perspective that encompasses a complex definition of the group and builds expectations about human behavior and feeling based on group-related responses. Alderfer has proposed this definition of a human group.

A human group is a collection of individuals (1) who have significant interdependent relations with each other, (2) who preceive themselves as a group by reliably distinguishing members from non-members, (3) who have differentiated roles in the group as a function of expectations from themselves, other group members and non-group members, and (4) who, as group members acting alone or in concert, have significantly interdependent relations with other groups.[8]

This definition of the human group implies consequences for individuals, group, and organizational behavior. For individuals, group membership provides meaning, location, and a sense of self-definition. Of course, individuals participate both consciously and unconsciously in multiple group memberships that in their complexity locate the individual in multidimensional space. According to this perspective, all interactions between groups are affected by the power relationships between the groups and by some degree of conflict. Group patterns of interaction with other groups emerge in a sociocultural context, a context partially defined by history. Therefore most current patterns of intergroup relations have their roots in history.

Differences between individuals and groups in race, sex, age, status, wealth, and power are traditional sources of intergroup dynamics. When these differences are combined, as they often are in organizations (where low-status occupations are filled by females, high-status by males), the potential dimensions of intergroup affect and behavior are complex and profound.[9]

As incoming representatives of an historically rooted intergroup relationship, the males and females in sex-atypical positions represented targets for some of the conflict that has characterized the relationship between males and females in a work situation. In these situations a New Type employee who enters a work group dominated by one sex in a sex-typed occupation is crossing more than one set of meaningful boundaries.

As representatives of the other sex, the incoming sex-atypical employee, especially a first or second arrival, has no recognized claim to membership and moreover represents a nonmember. In general,

theories about intergroup relationships contend that
nonmembers enable groups to define who they are in terms of boundaries that distinguish them from who they are not. This boundary definition is an important characteristic of human groups and of human systems in general, according to systems theorists.[10]

When a nonmember ("foreign" substance) enters a group, the nonmember acts as an irritant and represents a threat to individual and group definitions previously shared by members. The entry itself challenges the groups' self-definition. On the group and organizational level, an occupation or work group defined by its task, status, and sex composition can no longer be so readily identified once a new member of a different sex arrives. Similarly, on the individual level, belonging to an occupation implied that a person was competent at a task, represented a certain status, and was male or female. Such implications become incomplete with the addition of new and different members. Change in sex composition nudges change in group and individual self-definition for all parties.

Intergroup transactions, especially changes in membership, have meanings for group members. An intergroup transaction requires the articulation of new group boundaries, either temporarily or permanently. In this articulation, group members are caught in a dilemma that is inherent in the modification of familiar definitions and boundaries by the inclusion of a new member. As our study participants asked, "Can we still be ourselves?" On one level the question pertains to issues of decorum and conduct. On another level it is a question about group and individual self-definition, perhaps rephrased as, Who are we now? Anticipation of the arrival of a newcomer of a different stripe did stimulate apprehension among those in the host group. That apprehension reflected concerns about self- and group definitions, which had previously been grounded in shared characteristics of sex.

The group dilemma involves a balance between maintenance of the group's sense of itself in familiar terms, and organizational pressures to change the definition of who is within and who is outside the boundaries.

Perhaps one group solution to this dilemma is to identify the representative of the incoming "other" as slightly different from those presently in the group. In this way the other remains slightly outside group life; the other is marginal, as Hughes suggested, or is incorporated into the group situation in some way that is compatible with the group's and the individual's boundary definitions for itself and individuals. From this perspective, occupying the role of "token" may address the group's dilemma about boundary definition since it identifies the new member as different from others in the group but different in a way that is comfortable or predictable for that kind of person.

For example, we heard reports from women that men treated them like "mascots," maternal figures, "helpless and weak" individuals. Female New Types always reported these treatments as acts or examples of kindness by the men. These characterizations, almost caricatures of sex role stereotypes, are consistent with Kanter's designations of typical token roles for women—mother, sex object, pet, and "iron maiden."[11] An additional type might be the weakling or incompetent, an attribute frequently mentioned by men as an expectation and basis for behavior toward new female work group members. The men in women's jobs, on the other hand, frequently reported that they were treated like the boss or the manager, even as newcomers, and were expected to know more about the job than they felt was realistic based on their experience and training.

Both of the conditions are examples of "role encapsulation," which has been cited as one consequence of the token role[12] but which may actually be a more generic response to the dilemma faced by both individuals and work groups. Role encapsulation responds to the group's need to maintain familiar boundaries, a need that conflicts with the organizational requirement for change in work group membership. Role encapsulation, fitting the new group members into positions typical of their sex, enables the group to put them in their place and to maintain the semblance of a traditional sense of identification for members and group alike. This process is one response to the requirement that groups and occupations add new members. As a long-term "solution" to the dilemma of group and individual definitions, this response could become maladaptive, since it would continue to support a limited range of task-related and interpersonal behavior among group members. This limited range would tend to diminish the repertoire of member resources available to a work or occupational group and decrease individual and group productivity.

From earlier observations about sex composition and ratios, we might predict that role encapsulation would change as the proportion of the minority changes. Once group or occupational membership was somewhat balanced, role encapsulation would be a less prevalent form of adaptation to the group dilemma. Other forms of intergroup relationships might then occur with the formation of subgroups.

Theorists about group life have suggested that a universal state of anxiety characterizes the entry of newcomers into groups. The anxiety is felt by the newcomers, for whom issues of inclusion are elicited by the unfamiliar others. Anxiety is said to be felt by group members as well, when they are faced with a change in the familiar organization of their lives. Feelings of anxiety and strangeness are said to be features of a chronic human situation—the entry of a newcomer to an established situation. When that entry is exaggerated by a visible difference between the newcomer and the host group, both anxiety and response to it become more pronounced, thus raising more intense personal issues. The issues can be quickly resolved through the assumption of specific and predictable roles that reduce the threat to self-definition implied by the new situation. The issues can also be dealt with by striving for mastery, to prove through competence that one belongs.

The push for mastery or competence was experienced by both men and women New Types in this study. Similarly, there were suggestions from both about the adoption of a prototypical male or female role in the new situation and the expectation shared with other members of the work group that they would fulfill the role and carry out certain behaviors.

Although there were differences between them in form and substance, the men and women New Types shared certain propensities in response to the anxiety of entry. On the other hand, there also appeared to be differences between the men and women in the kinds of entry experience and feeling they mentioned to us.

One explanation of entry experience differences between male and female New Types is offered by Alderfer's theory of "embedded intergroups."[13] This theory views the individual and the immediate work group as components of larger systems that can be described in terms of dominant features, values, emphases, and groups. The values and emphases of the larger system surround each succeeding smaller system that encloses the individual and immediate work group. This surrounding affects the transactions between the individual and his or her work group, between work groups, between work groups and larger work units, and so on. The theory predicts that a representative of the dominant values or dominant group would be more readily received in a smaller unit (work group) than a representative of the non-dominant group. For this reason a male newcomer to a female work group that operates in an environment characterized by male dominance would be accepted more readily than a female newcomer to a male group that operates in the same environment. Since the organization in this study is characterized by a male-dominated hierarchy, we would predict that males would be more readily accepted into female work groups or, conversely, that there would be more resistance to female entry into a male work group. These predictions are borne out by this study's findings.

Confirmation of this hypothesis is the difference between men and women New Types in their reports of the amount of time it took them to fit in after they had moved into their new work groups. The New Type women reported that the time it took them to fit in was longer than that reported for the average male employee in the male group. The male New Types, on the other hand, sensed that it took them less time to fit in than it did female newcomers.

Summary

The comments and observations of men and women who moved into New Type work situations reveal that such movement meant change for newcomer and host group. This change and its anticipation stimulated questions about group and self-identity, questions that can be interpreted as expressions of an intergroup relationship and of an intergroup transaction in which there was a transposition of the New Type employee into a Same Type host group. This transposition was viewed as a dilemma of group and individual self-definition for all parties.

Because the transposition was required by organizational mandate, this dilemma required adaptation on the part of all participants. This discussion identified some of the kinds of adaptation reported by study participants and highlighted the phenomenon of the token role, extra pressure to prove oneself on the job, and the process of role encapsulation. These concepts are again addressed in discussions of another facet of this new work experience.

5 MOVING ON: GOALS AND ROLES

With the effort to increase work opportunities for men, women, and minority group members, the federal government has sought to influence both hiring and promotion procedures in organizations. By monitoring promotion practices, government agencies have attempted to induce organizations to modify structural constraints that have frequently limited organizational members to specific kinds of job or organizational location. Organizations have most recently been required to create new promotion mechanisms, incentives, and opportunities for women and minorities.

While neither emphasis on nor value of upward mobility may be shared by all employees, equal opportunity for such mobility has recently been assumed to be a civil right. Opportunity structures have been studied by social and political observers; in general they have been viewed as important determinants of organizational and social behavior. From this perspective one facet of an operational definition of opportunity structure derives from individual thoughts about promotion. Individual perceptions of an opportunity structure are most intriguing in a situation where traditional mobility paths may not be perceived as appropriate for nontraditional employees. For all the New Types, occupancy of their jobs represented an organizational (and personal) effort to counteract traditional opportunity patterns and to occupy positions previously barred to members of one sex. Once these positions have been occupied, what next?

As we noted in chapter 4 there were similar responses to questions about entry and job occupancy from both male and female New Types, but there were also striking differences between the two groups. One notable attitudinal difference between them centered on perceptions of their futures in the organization and expectations about promotion. The study initially addressed many questions about promotion and vertical mobility—expectations, behavior, satisfactions. These practical questions elicited diverse responses that clearly differentiated be-

tween the men and women in the study and particularly between the men and women in New Type positions.

Before the Job: Hopes and Dreams?

All the participants were questioned about their work
plans, past, current, and future. For example, we
asked, What work would you do if you could start
again? What would you do if you could afford to quit
working today? Two questions helped characterize
employees' expectations when they began work in
the company: The first question was, When you first
came to the company, was there a job you wanted to
get to? The responses to this question are shown in
table 12. There is more similarity among the males,
no matter what their jobs, than among the men and
women in either sex-typical or sex-atypical positions.
Most men had jobs they wanted when they first came
to the company; most women did not. The second
question, Now is there a job you want? elicited the
responses presented in table 13. Comparison between tables 12 and 13 indicates that the proportion
of women who have their sights set on a job in the
company has increased. As table 13 suggests, there is

TABLE 12

Was There a Job You Wanted?

	Same Types		New Types	
	Females	Males	Females	Males
Yes	7	18	6	17
No	18	7	19	7

Table 13

Is There a Job You Want Now?

	Same Types		New Types	
	Females	Males	Females	Males
Yes	16	20	14	25
No	9	5	11	0

no clear-cut difference between male and female Same Types in their interests in other jobs in the company, but there is a difference between male and female New Types in the specificity of their future job interests. The New Type women have lower expectations about futures in the company than members of any other group, and they have significantly lower expectations than their male counterparts who hold typically female jobs, in terms of interest in a specific company job.

Before the Job: Why?

Differences in expectations about jobs in the organization were also reflected in the reasons that individuals took jobs. The responses to the question, Why did you take this job? were clustered into four categories, each representing a set of motives or intentions. The responses to this question are shown in table 14.

Comments about why they took the job amplified the specific reasons offered by these employees.

Table 14
Why Did You Take This Job?

	Same Types		New Types	
	Females	Males	Females	Males
More pay	7	7	6	6
Promotion (job itself) or as part of move up	1	8	3	9
Learn new skills, different or more appropriate work	9	10	10	10
Disliked old job	7	0	6	0
	25	25	25	25

From male New Types we heard:

I knew I'd have a better chance for promotion in this job.

I wanted to better myself in experience, to give myself a base for promotion. I don't think it's really a man's job, so I wouldn't think of staying too long.

I took this for a knowledge of the company and the different promotions available here. I could move to a lot of jobs from this one and know more about them.

The women offered different explanations:

I hated my old job and would have taken anything to get out of it.

This job offered much higher pay than the one I had before, so there was no question in my mind. Besided I didn't like the other one.

My supervisor really encouraged me to take this job; and she didn't have to work too hard to persuade me. The pay was better, and my old job was awful—both in the work and in the hours. There was no question in my mind about making the move.

I was hoping to learn some new skills and to get some work that would get me moving more. I like to move around a lot more than I like sitting at a desk.

Once again reasons given for entering the present job are more similar among the males and among the females than among the occupants of New Type or Same Type positions. Most of the males in sex-atypical positions took their jobs for purposes of upward movement. This reason was also offered by some of the men in sex-typical positions, though not quite as many. But only four women mentioned promotion as a reason for taking their jobs, while seventeen men gave promotion as the reason. No men said that they had disliked their old jobs, while thirteen (25 percent) of the women gave this as a reason. Of the other reasons, pay was mentioned equally frequently for all categories of employees. Wanting a "different kind of work experience" was mentioned most frequently by those who moved into New Type positions, especially the females.

In sum, the males, especially the male New Types, see their present jobs as part of a move upward in the company. Very few of the females share that view. The females' reasons for moving into the job were either dislike of a previous job, interest in trying a new job, or better pay.

After the Job

Everyone was asked, Does your job offer many or few opportunities for the future? Responses were coded along a five-point continuum: none, few, some, many, very many (table 15). Both females in Same Type jobs and the males in New Type jobs (these are the same jobs) saw many future possibilities coming from their current jobs. Males in Same Type jobs and females in New Type jobs saw fewer opportunities following their current positions (the same jobs). Earlier analysis indicated that females in New Type positions and males in Same Type positions had depressed expectations about their futures in this company at this time. The significance of these differences between the groups may be influenced by the effect of the one "vulnerable" job included in the study. Still, that job can account for only 24 responses (12 male and 12 female) of the 31 (14 from women and 17 from men) most negative responses to this question.

Table 15
Future Possibilities

	Same Types		New Types	
	Females	Males	Females	Males
None	0	7	5	3
Few	4	10	9	1
Some	2	2	5	2
Many	5	3	1	4
Very Many	14	3	5	15

The differences between males as a group and females as a group remain notable.

In a subsequent question, we asked everyone, What do you expect to be doing after you leave this job? Their responses were broken down into four categories (table 16). Consistent with their responses to other questions about postjob plans and expectations, the New Type males reported the highest expectations about staying in the organization and less uncertainty about the future than any other group. Equivalent numbers of females reported plans to leave work for family responsibility. The responses to the question about a future in the organization show greater similarity among females, whether New Type or Same Type, than among males and females in New Type positions. These data show that there is more parallel or symmetry between three groups; the two female groups and the group of males in sex-typical jobs, all of whom differ from the male New Types. Again the males in New Type positions expect to remain in the organization. Other groups are less certain, perhaps reflecting an ambiguity of future opportunity that seems to be related to sex or job type.

After the Job: Schemes

One way to learn more about aspirations is by studying the behaviors related to their realization. Fortunately some of this information is available through data generated by the study.

In a question designed to meet the organization's personnel interests, all employees were asked whether they had talked about their future work plans with anyone in the company. This question was expected to elicit descriptive data that could be used by the organization to assess managerial effectiveness in employee career counseling. The question provided information useful for the organization, as well as information about the sample group and inherent differences in future-oriented organizational activities. The responses to this question are shown in table 17.

Table 16

After This Job

	Same Types		New Types	
	Females	Males	Females	Males
Another Job in Company	10	12	13	23
Another Job Outside	2	5	1	0
Home with Family	5	0	5	0
Uncertain	8	8	6	2

Table 17

Talk about Future Work Plans

	Same Types		New Types	
	Females	Males	Females	Males
Yes	11	17	6	23
No	14	8	19	2

There was no important difference between men and women in Same Type positions when talking about future plans. For the men and women in New Type positions, however, the difference is dramatic. The females in sex-atypical positions very often answered no to this question. It is difficult to interpret the meaning of this finding without more information about the process of career discussion: Who usually initiates such discussions, the supervisor or the employee? No matter what the procedure, women in the sex-atypical jobs have not been talking about their futures in the company with anyone. Even the females in sex-typical jobs have talked more about their futures than their New Type counterparts. Most of the men (78 percent) have spoken with someone about their futures in the company. Almost all the men in sex-atypical positions have spoken to someone about their futures, even more frequently than have their counterparts in sex-typical male jobs.

Before and after the Job: Themes

Some themes that emerge from these descriptive analyses seem to reinforce patterns mentioned earlier. The contrasts between men and women in the New Type jobs are overshadowed by the overall differences between men and women in all jobs studied, at least in terms of expectations, approach, and continuing plans about job and position in the organization. The men seem to be more focused on a future in the organization and have been since their initial entry to the company, according to their reports. The women tend to show a consistently different attitude toward career plans; the New Type women seem both most pessimistic about future opportunities and least active about discussing future opportunities with someone at the company. The male New Types are both optimistic and active.

These patterns are corroborated by themes expressed in the interview material. When asked why they think a man would want a "woman's job," most women thought that for men it was a stepping-stone on the career ladder (73 percent of the female respondents named this reason); thus they shared the men's rationale for taking such positions. There was much more uncertainty among both men and women about why a woman would want a man's job (64 percent said "I don't know") in response to this question. How can this difference in attitude, affect, and behavior be understood?

Discussion

The differences between men and women in their attitudes toward futures in the organization are most dramatically expressed by men and women in New Type positions. Here is a group of optimistic, planning males in contrast to a female group characterized by ambiguous expectations and little activity about an organizational future.

Almost everyone interviewed agreed that men take women's jobs to have a stepping-stone in the organization. New Type men saw their clerical positions as white-collar and as first steps in a movement toward management positions.

Such expectations about movement into management positions for males who begin in clerical jobs are not based on actual movements and trends, at least for the three years for which personnel data was available. Appendix F shows overall and specific patterns. No men moved up from three of the clerical jobs in 1974, 1975, or 1976, although in 1976 one man moved into a lower-level job. In the largest clerical category in our study and in the company as a whole in 1974, nine of the males in the job left it; eight left the company and one moved into a lower-level position within the company. In 1975 ten males moved out of the job, four (40 percent) into higher-level positions, three into lower-level positions, and three out of the organization. In 1975 more men moved down or out than up. In 1976, when this study was conducted, fourteen men left this job, seven (50 percent) into higher-level jobs and the other seven into lower-level jobs or out of the organization. If these numbers are correct, then expectations about movement upward in the organization for males in clerical jobs are not based on the actual movement patterns of men in these positions. More recent trends seem to show that men in this job are now faring better, but these trends do not seem extensive enough to support the pervasive career explanations and expectations of the males in clerical positions.

To explain the extent of these expectations, it is important to look first to the general organizational situation for clues to the beliefs expressed by the sample. The majority of white-collar management positions are occupied by men, and in the past, males who moved into management positions as supervisors of clerical workers often spent short periods of time in the clerical position to learn something about it. Only those who had been in the organization for more than ten years mentioned this practice to the investigator, so it would not be a convenient explanation for the expectations among younger people. Situational information provides some evidence to explain the belief that men can move up from clerical positions, but there is not quite enough evidence to be satisfying.

Tradition: Ambition

In the discussion of moving in, I introduced two concepts to explain some of the attitudes and behavior accompanying the entry of New Type employees to the host group: role encapsulation and the differential effect of intergroup transactions on group and individual behavior and affect. Together these concepts provide some understanding of the differences in organizational goals for men and women in sex-atypical positions.

In the earlier discussion I suggested that one response to the difficulty of being the token might be role encapsulation, where individuals in these positions take on the stereotypical characteristics of the group that they represent in the intergroup situation. Role encapsulation responds to both group and individual dilemmas about self-definition and provides a shared response to this dilemma for host group and newcomer alike. The dramatic emphasis of the males in sex-atypical positions on their futures in the organization may be a form of role encapsulation manifest in the exaggeration of the stereotypically male emphasis on achievement in work.[1] Men in American society, according to some observers, view work as a proving ground, as an opportunity for self-validation through competition and success. Moving within an organization to positions of higher status has been described as a compelling pull on men, a direction for

which they have been socialized from early child-
hood. From the perspective of role encapsulation,
then, it would make sense that the men in token positions within women's occupations might exaggerate
their upward motivation and mobility and that this
exaggeration would be supported by both the newcomer male and the host group females. The belief in
male ambition is shared by both males and females,
and in this respect it can fulfill needs for individual and
group boundary clarity. If the men are moving upward,
as men should, then they will move into positions of
authority, where they belong; they will not remain at
the lower levels typically occupied by females, who
belong there. Such token male roles as achievers and
bosses may represent counterparts to female roles as
mascot, seductress, iron maiden, and mother.

This explanation of role encapsulation is stimulated
by the persistence of the sex-atypical male's optimism about promotion, despite the paucity of
specific evidence of promotions and despite supervisory evaluations that generally disagree with these
beliefs. The need to sustain a view of oneself as am-
bitious and striving, perhaps different from the
women with whom one works, may also fulfill a personal need for cognitive consistency around sex role
identity, since it provides a self-view that is consonant
with an important feature of "maleness."

The New Type women provide an interesting contrast to the males' beliefs, attitudes, and behavior in
relation to upward mobility. These women have such
limited views of their own futures in the organization
that their perspective also compels some explanation.
Perhaps they are responding to an organizational
situation where they are promoted neither within
their own job categories nor through them to managerial positions. After all, the members of this group
have remained in their jobs longer than the men in
comparable positions. They may stay longer because
they are successful in their jobs, because there is no

actual opportunity to move up, or because they perceive that there is no opportunity for upward movement. The organizational situation offers few examples of women who have moved into the upper ranks of nonmanagement and management jobs; thus an inability to conceive of the possibility of moving up would be a realistic response to the organizational situation.

Another interpretation of this female self-view is possible, since there are indications of some comparability to the male role encapsulation process within this group. Perhaps the women who have moved into the male jobs have moved into encapsulated or exaggerated female roles, where the exaggeration expresses itself in a lack of ambition and career orientation, a position and orientation for which many women have been socialized. It may be that nonassertive behavior around future careers in the organization is a function of the view of females in male jobs shared by the men and women alike: No matter how well they do this job, they are still not cut out to move up. Women belong in the lower strata of the organization, just as men belong in the upper strata.

Such a contention meshes with the previous discussion of the intergroup and leads to another set of observations about cognitive dissonance. Thus far I have focused on transition and transposition to sex-atypical jobs as horizontal movement from one group to another without considering the vertical properties of such moves. These vertical properties pertain to questions of status and relative position in a hierarchy. There *is* a difference between men and women in this study in the jobs they have occupied and their place in the organizational heirarchy. This difference manifests itself in various forms. First, all the male jobs are higher in the organizational hierarchy than any of the female jobs selected for inclusion in the study, a phenomenon that reflects a larger social and occupational pattern.

Thus women who have moved into male jobs have moved up from their usual positions in women's jobs. The men who took women's jobs did not actually move down because most were in lower-paying and lower-status jobs previously. Still a female clerical job is a lower position than the usual positions of men in this organization and in the occupational world in general. Thus New Type men are in positions lower than those in which they would expect to find themselves, while New Type women are in positions higher than those in which they would expect to find themselves. The men's descriptions of their experiences of extra pressure offer testimony of their lower positions. Their concerns are related to differentiating themselves from the women in the jobs and to clarifying their higher expectations; they tend not to worry about acceptance by peers or ability to do the job.

Both men and women exemplify the status incongruencies as a potential source of stress and distress for individuals. This situation provides examples of two types of status incongruence. The move from a higher-status to a lower-status position is more difficult than the move from a lower- to a higher-status position, although both moves subject the individual to cognitive dissonance because there is a discrepancy between an individual's self-view and his or her position in a hierarchy.

Theorists of cognitive dissonance have identified a range of potential individual responses to this condition, responses that include the perceptual, behavioral, and the affective. One particularly salient response identified by an anthropologist-psychologist team, links theories of intergroup behavior and cognitive dissonance.[2]

Anthropological evidence suggests that when groups move into "lower positions [in the occupational structure] dissonant with their previous self-image,"[3] particular responses ensue. These authors propose that such groups and their individual members try to reduce cognitive dissonance by trying to move up within the occupational structure. Specific conditions determine the selection of this response to dissonance for a particular group, but the proposition rests squarely on cognitive dissonance theory. Essentially, the theory proposes, one way to restore consistency between one's self-view and the occupancy of an unexpectedly low position in a hierarchy is to focus on moving up in the heirarchy and to organize one's behavior toward this end. Such an orientation has been observed by anthropologists in studies of tribal behavior.[4]

In support of this theoretical application is evidence that one of the major differences between the males and females in sex-atypical positions has been their orientation to and expectations about upward movement. The males are in positions lower than their previous self-image allows; they are in female-typed clerical jobs, which usually occupy the lowest strata of an organizational or occupational hierarchy. Just as moving up has been emphasized by the men in women's clerical jobs, so it has been emphasized for men in social work.

Males adjust to the problems of being a male minority in a female profession by choosing fields of practice and practice methods which are more characteristically sex-typed, and by moving up to administrative positions in the professional hierarchy.[5]

With a slight change in emphasis, one can argue that moving up is characteristic of men in a woman's occupation. It is not the particular choice of specialty within the occupation that is sex-typed; rather, it is the position of that choice relative to the status of men and women in the culture at large and within a particular organization or occupation.

An orientation toward moving up may resolve two issues at once for the individual. It enables the individual to maintain a self-consistent view of himself while occupying a position dissonant with his expectations. He can also direct himself toward movement out of the dissonant position into a position more consonant with his self-view. This is not to say that psychological consistency or upward mobility are intrinsically positive ends; rather that process is one response to a situation characterized by status inconsistency.

Alternative explanations for male-female differences in orientations to work and career have frequently been considered in the literature. Such explanations include sex-role socialization, often favored by psychologists, and structural explanations of responses to blocked mobility, often favored by sociologists. In adding hypotheses about intergroup transactions, status inconsistency, and dissonance reduction to the interpretations of individual behavior in these situations, I have suggested a potential area for further conceptual and empirical exploration as well as a potential resource for individual and organizational change.

6 CHANGING PLACES:
CONCLUSIONS AND IMPLICATIONS

In this description of a contemporary social phenomenon, I have presented a picture of changing places in which men and women have moved into positions that previously excluded or limited participation by members of their sex. In this description of a complex organizational situation, I have described changing places from still another perspective. Here are work places that are changing in response to environmental demands in terms of technology, economic pressure, and governmental requirement. These changes, exerted through pressure on the organization at large, pulsate through it and change the shape of the work environment for individuals and groups. Thus, as men and women are changing jobs, their jobs, work groups, and work situations are changing as well. In acknowledging those changes I have sought to explicate the intersecting effects of different forms and magnitudes of change and to develop ways of understanding how these effects impinge on individual work lives.

The focus has required kaleidoscopic vision. The more information I acquired about the environment, the more multifaceted became the research sights, questions, and strategies. Complicated questions merited sophisticated analyses and in turn generated the need for tools different from those with which the exploration began.

Perhaps the most useful way to appreciate the final shape of this work is to view it as a source of personal and aggregate information about a contemporary social experience that was also connected to a recent organizational intervention. Both experience and intervention are embedded in a larger social context alive with political, social, and economic forces that all converge in the personal lives glimpsed through the research. Because the work entailed some description and analysis of a contemporary social-organizational intervention, some of its characteristics are similar to characteristics of social policy, experimentation, and research. Since a social innovation, by definition, marks an effort to deal with previously unsolved social problems, it is an exploratory move, "a collective venture into the unknown." Because answers are not available beforehand and because of the complexities of actual experimentation in the real world, one must adopt an unorthodox epistemological stance, one that tolerates "a backward progression from what appear to be self-evident ideas about social problems and remedies through perplexing program results, to ever more fundamental inquiries about program assumptions and society."[1]

Self-Evident Ideas

This project was built on a cluster of "self-evident ideas" about the nature of sex-typed work and the meaning of changes in this work for individuals and organizations. Conceptual links were originally drawn from a host of resources to document the contention that individual movement into and occupancy of a different sex-typed job would be a stress condition for those individuals. Among the resources that supported this contention were descriptive portrayals from specific professional literatures, social science studies and documents, and a compilation of theories about personal social comparison processes, intergroup behavior, and the token position. These resources led me to expect a difference between the work experiences of New Types and those of Same Types.

In the systematic pursuit of these theoretically based propositions, it became apparent that other conditions were operant in this work situation and that these conditions—also associated with change—could have an impact on the employees included in the original study. The discovery that other immediate and impending job-related changes were associated with one of the jobs in the study made necessary to identify at least two sources of change and subsequent stress conditions for employees.

Statistical analyses helped me examine the panoply of forces impinging on these workers' lives and thus provided useful situational diagnostic information. The statistical tools also facilitated consideration of more theoretical questions pertinent to this situation and questions previously neglected in stress-related theory and research.

Stress-Related Theory

These results suggest two important contributions to stress-related research. First, there may be a connection between stress and work satisfaction. New Type employees express more satisfaction with their work than Same Type employees. This finding was clarified through statistical analyses that showed that the New Type employees in the two least satisfying jobs were more positive than their Same Type peers about work itself. I speculated that this difference might be related to choosing a job based on ability rather than sex and the connection between stress, extra effort at the job (for which the study provided strong evidence about the New Types), challenge, commitment to work, and work satisfaction. The relationship between challenge, commitment to work, and work satisfaction has been proposed by those who have most recently developed theoretical approaches to the understanding of work satisfaction. A third theoretical explanation derives from Selye's contentions about the positive effects of a counterstress in an already stressful situation, especially a chronically disabling situation such as a tense, demanding, or boring job. That the New Type men and women in the least satisfying jobs expressed more work satisfaction than their peers was surprising but consistent with Selye's theory. Certainly no conclusive theoretical statements can be made on the basis of a single research effort, yet material for continued theoretical exploration and development has been offered.

Other Theoretical Implications

Although I did not rely on assumptions about "sex role" in carrying out this study, the results have raised some questions about connections between job, position, and expectations about sex-related role behavior. I have used group-intergroup and cognitive dissonance theory to interpret the expectations and behavior of men and women in New Type positions. This interpretation suggests that current sex-role related behaviors and expectations may have crystallized from expectations and norms connected with historical social positions.[2] These norms and expectations may have been transformed into fairly stable contemporary role-related expectations about behaviors. Once sex-role related behaviors and expectations have been internalized through the socialization process, they become reflexive role expectations, an internal set of guidelines for behavior shared by males and females about themselves and each other. Thus what may have begun as a contingency of social position at another time is carried on as a *fact* of sex-role identification and expectations about others. Such identifications are clearly influenced, shaped, and redetermined by contemporary situations.

The thrust and direction of this research emphasizes the contingencies of social position as a source of sex role-specific expectations about behavior. Nothing that I have heard or learned reduces my appreciation of the effect of social situational characteristics rather than personality or trait descriptors as a dominant influence on organizational behavior. Emphasis on the contingencies of situation more than personality, genetic differences, or early socialization is a characteristic of the most recent theory and research about men and women in organizations.[3] This situational orientation, while intellectually appealing, is far more difficult to grasp empirically and challenges us to make more tangible connections between theory and evidence.

This general perspective also encompasses the theoretical explanations that helped me interpret some of the similarities and differences between male and female New Type personal and work group experiences. Similarities in these experiences may come from a common position as lone or rare representative in an intergroup transaction or, in other words, occupancy of a token position. Thus expectations, attitudes, and behaviors attached to this position may be exaggerated by all parties because the person in that position represents more than himself or herself in the group situation. That person represents a history of transactions between two groups, a history that is bound to have an impact on the current situation. No matter who the individuals are, nor what personal qualities they bring to a situation, they represent more than themselves to the other members of that work group. Thus they raise a question about group identity that is not raised when a Same Type person enters the new work situation.

While there were visible similarities between the experiences of men and women in New Type jobs, there were differences as well. Despite the efforts to control differences in rank between male and female jobs in this situation, no effort could counteract organizational reality or make the jobs studied completely comparable. Lack of comparability between male and female jobs reflects a stable historical trend that emphasizes the higher status and prestige usually attributed to "male" jobs in this society. From the outset, then, the male and female New Type experiences could not be viewed as completely comparable because it was impossible to assert that their jobs were completely comparable on all dimensions. With this fact as backgroiund, there are hints of other differences, between the experiences of male and female New Types that merit attention.

The New Type movements described here are not only horizontal occupational movements but vertical as well. These men and women have not been moving only across lines of difference between jobs and activities, they have been moving up and down between positions at different levels. Thus the New Types are located in places different from those they might have anticipated and at levels of the organization different from those that might be expected of their sex. Finding oneself at a level different from that of similar others requires one to reconcile the difference between expectation and actuality. What has been called "status inconsistency" can create a form of cognitive dissonance for the individual. The state of cognitive dissonance, according to most social psychologists, is so uncomfortable that the individual attempts to rectify or change the situation through a cognitive, affective, or behavioral shift. Thus the individual may change values or feelings about the dissonance-evoking situation ("My job isn't *that* important"), or the individual may attempt to change the inconsistent situation by trying to get out of it. The New Type men in pink-collar jobs may be attempting through affect, belief, and behavior to change their work situations, which place them lower in the hierarchy of organizational and occupational prestige than they as males may have anticipated. By viewing their jobs as stepping-stones to management, by feeling that their time in the job is short and that they are headed for higher positions in the organization, by setting their sights on the higher opportunities and discussing these opportunities with supervisors, these men have been working cognitively, affectively, and behaviorally to rectify a situation dissonant with their expectations. Men are "supposed to be" in higher positions in organizational hierarchies and in higher-status occupations. When they find themselves in lower organizational positions or in lower-status occupations, they may cope through plans to move up to positions in which they "belong."

Clearly there are other plausible interpretations of the attitudes, expectations, and behaviors of the male New Types. The organization may have encouraged them to take their jobs by promising or hinting at promotions. Supervisors may treat them differently and act differently toward them on the basis of their views. Because company promotion statistics are not generally known in the company, it is understandable that men would be naive about the actual promotion rates from their jobs. Whatever the explanation, their personal expectations appear discrepant from the actual pattern of upward movement in this organization. Similar expectations, attitudes, and behaviors toward upward movement have been observed and documented in female-typed occupations such as nursing and social work as well as in a parallel tribal situation[4] of status discrepancy. The combination of parallel situations creates a compelling set of theoretical arguments that merit further attention.

The situation of the New Type women provokes similar theoretical and empirical follow-up. Their similarities to the New Type males have been described and analyzed. Their differences, especially concerning expectations for the future, have been documented. The empirical evidence suggests that the female New Types have limited expectations about moving up in this organization, had not considered this an important facet of their initial job change, and were not focused either affectively, cognitively, or behaviorally on changing their place or level in the organization. Perhaps people who occupy positions that are better or higher than those they believe they should hold respond to the dissonance by focusing on holding on to their positions, on remaining at the level they have reached. This reasoning may explain in part the pressure that the female New Types felt to prove that they belonged where they were. Doubts about making it in a job would be stronger if one felt that one had moved higher than one should. Similarly, we might interpret the report of the female New Types that it took them longer to fit in in terms of the feeling of not belonging at a higher than expected level in an organizational or occupational structure. Thus status inconsistency and accompanying cognitive dissonance for the female New Types might stimulate behavior directed toward holding on to the job, say working hard. When the discrepancy between person and place is negative, when the person is in a position higher than might be expected, that person may feel the need to make up the difference between expected and actual position.[5]

In sum, two sets of theoretical perspectives have offered insights to these findings. Stress-related theory and some of its offshoots help explain unusual patterns of difference between those in New Type and those in Same Type jobs. This study's findings could amplify and enrich the body of empirical work connected to stress-related theory. A second area of theoretical insight demanding more development based on current findings is that which focuses on the relationship between group-intergroup phenomena and connects with individual attitudes, feelings, and behavior. One plausible link among these three areas of analysis was suggested through the application of cognitive dissonance theory to the situation of employees whose organizational positions created conditions of status inconsistency. More such applications and developments are possible and necessary.

Ever More Fundamental Inquiries

What kinds of question have been posed and not fully addressed by the work so far? What kinds of question might be reformulated now, knowing what we know about the people and perspectives? Most research reports end with the conventional more-questionsthan-answers statement, and this report is no exception.

Among the unanswered questions are specific inquiries about work group composition, majorityminority proportions, and individual majorityminority member interaction, affect, and behavior. As a microcosm of organizational life, the work groups

and their members offered rich but uneven information about intragroup behavior and the meaning of
membership for individuals. Are there differences in
individual experiences in groups of differing sex
compositions? Recent laboratory research suggests
that there are measurable differences in individual
experiences and social attributions for majority and
minority group members when group racial composition is altered.[6] Does this hold for sex composition?
Does the passage of time, difficult to map in the laboratory research setting, modify this effect?

The question of work group composition and its
effects leads to questions with more global implications. What about the sex composition of occupations: Is there a relationship between occupational
sex composition, individual expectations, and organizational behavior? A specific example of this effect
is demonstrated in this study. There seems to be a
common expectation for men in occupations that are
female sex-typed and have greater proportions of
female members to feel and behave in a consistent
manner. Are there similar, discernible themes attached to the direction, expectations and behavior of
women in occupations sex-typed as male and occupied largely by men? One way to pursue these
questions is to undertake a systematic search of occupational literatures with content analysis of their
treatment of the minority sex in editorials, journal
coverage, and the substance of published research.

Related to these questions are questions about sex
composition of organizational hierarchical strata and
individual expectations and behavior. Do the effects
of sex composition and proportion on the individual
depend on the hierarchical position of his or her job?
For example, the jobs represented here spanned a
somewhat limited range of positions in the organizational hierarchy. It would be interesting to sample a
broader range of levels and jobs to determine
whether there is a difference in New Type expectations and affective responses to jobs that can be ex-

plained by the combination of organizational level and proportion of majority to minority members at particular levels. Which of these organizational characteristics is more influential in the explanation of individual New Type perceptions, affect, expectations, and behavior in relation to a future in the organization, as well as current satisfaction with work?

There are also the perennial questions of demography. Is there a difference between New Type and Same Type employees in individual and demographic characteristics that has not been explicated so far? Are there differences in characteristics such as education, parents' educational and occupational levels, marriage, children, and spouse's educational and occupational levels? These questions can be considered through continuing analysis of the study's data. The answers to other questions depend on more extensive data collection within this organization and beyond.

A few of these questions are important for practice and policy. What are the characteristic work experiences of men and women who leave sex-atypical jobs? Can organizational contributions to successful selection and placement be identified? If organizational contributions such as supervisor preparation, facilitation through supervisory or peer training, and the optimal sex compositon of a work group can be identified, they can be replicated systematically in this organization and in others as well. The organization in this study has initiated such an effort in relation to males in one clerical position, and their turnover rates for men in the position seem to have changed since then.

For the second major research undertaking, I recommend a longitudinal study of the employees who participated in this study. A first step would include follow-up for the current cohort of research participants at six-month intervals for the next five years to determine their affective responses to current jobs and their career development patterns, comparing

Same Type and New Type males and females.
Another longitudinal study might compare the entry
experiences of New Type employees and Same Type
employees who began work during the same period.
Such research seems to have been initiated at the
U.S. service academies and has been recommended
by scholars interested in organizational socialization.[7]
The feedback and publicity from these applied research projects may change the experience of subsequent New Type organizational members and thus
may make present and future research somewhat less
purely "scientific." This is one of the perils of applied
research in the social policy area. Still all these efforts
will refine and amplify theory developed thus far, as
will each version of the social experiment and piece of
social reform. Each attempted remedy and perplexing
program result adds to our knowledge, understanding, and capability for change.

Self-Evident Remedies?

In this case the self-evident ideas about social problems and remedies took the form of Affirmative Action plans that encouraged changes in hiring, accompanied by some efforts to remove the sex-typed
labels attached to particular jobs. Clearly these plans
and the organizational efforts to implement them
have made some changes in the work lives of most of
the people we met.

How much these changes actually address some of
the deep-rooted issues of organizational structure,
power, and hierarchy is not clear. Nor is it clear how
much these changes actually affect the lives of these
people. Where will the New Type men be five years
from now? Where will the New Type women be five
years from now? Will they have moved to positions
within the organization that support, encourage, and
challenge their skills, or will they be in the same jobs
(or lower jobs than) they occupy now? Will the pink-
collar become a white-collar for the young men who

view it as such? Will the blue-collar stay blue, or will changes in technology eradicate the need for blue-collar work and leave many New Type women and their male colleagues with the choice of a pink collar or the colorless coverall of a domestic service worker (janitor)?

These questions suggest implications for organizational policy and practice. Some aspects of what has been learned have more immediate diagnostic consequences for this organization and some implications for other similar organizations. Other features of the work are more readily generalizable to test and exploration in different organizations.

What I propose as implications for policy, program development, and resources planning are based on the assumption that it is beneficial (and legally necessary) for work organizations to offer equal opportunity to individuals to take positions for which they demonstrate qualifications, at any level of an organization; to be effective in these positions; to remain in these positions for periods optimal for themselves and the organization; and to have choices about leaving the positions, choices that maximize the fit between the individual's needs, preferences, and skills and the organization's current and future personnel requirements.

Based on such admittedly value-laden assumptions, I propose policy recommendations that apply to a particular organization but can be generalized to any other organization, with some modifications based on situational specifics. By now, it should be clear that these policy recommendations have blossomed from the original interest in the sex-typing of jobs and the effect of changing job sex-type on individuals and organizations. The larger issues of more pervasive influence that emerged in the study have influenced my view about the most important organizational patterns operating for this group of employees. Clearly the research project demonstrated that change of job sex-type was not a pervasive source of distress to study participants (employees). Of far more affective and behavioral import were issues about impending job loss. Acknowledging the magnitude of this effect led to the formulation of policy recommendations that address and extend the original focus of the study.

Less Evident Remedies

A most evident recommendation is that this organization continue its effort to support the assumption of sex-atypical jobs. In addition, the male and female New Type's positive work outcomes might be expected to appear in other organizations as well were we to use the same systematic methods to gather evidence. Given that these positive outcomes would be expected under similar work and research circumstances, it is possible to encourage other organizations to promote sex-atypical job occupancy. Overall effects seem to enhance individual and group work life.

For this organization and others, I offer a caveat before blanket encouragement. One study does not provide enough understanding about the long-term efficiency and effectiveness of a social intervention to prove its value. So it is important to undertake more studies of this phenomenon to delve into thorny questions raised here. What are the actual rates of retention for New Types in all jobs? Who is leaving which jobs, when, and why? In other words, a broader sample of organizations, organizational levels, jobs, and individuals would provide the full-fledged support needed for unqualified recommendation of the current policy or for the suggestion that it be expanded or discontinued.

Still another thorny consideration in the offer of blanket recommendation stems from this study's depiction of the entry of male and female New Type employees into new work settings. Originally theory about intergroup transactions led to questions about the entry experience. The eloquent personal testimony that these questions evoked from respondents made it clear that the entry experience for the New Type newcomer was different from and often more difficult than that of the Same Type newcomer. Moreover empirical evidence and theory suggest that this experience is generally more difficult for the female New Type than for the male. If entry is more difficult for the New Type employee, and especially for the female New Type employee, this is a fact of organizational (intergroup) life. Recognizing this fact would alert organizations to the need for resources to facilitate entry, to prevent high casualty rates among New Types, and to ease the long-term effect of transitions for those who succeed. The entry experience may contribute to the difficulties of the female New Types in their consideration of upward movement in the organization. I have suggested that female New Types may not be able to gather the momentum necessary to move up in the organization because they have had to expend so much time and energy to make it in their current jobs. Although the connections I have made between job entry and future plans are somewhat speculative, it is not speculation to note that the entry process is demanding, especially so for female New Types. If the entry process could be eased, by preparing newcomers, by having outside support groups, by making supervisors more sensitive, by moving in clusters or groups at the same time, then these work transitions and transpositions might be less immediately disruptive for everyone involved in them.

There is still another caveat to accompany the endorsement of current policies that encourage the assumption of sex-atypical jobs, specifically through Affirmative Action programs. If female and minority employees are directed toward jobs with predictably short organizational life spans, the contention of equal opportunity becomes less credible unless there is corresponding planning for promotion or future organizational opportunity for these employees. Although EEOC requirements may in time relax and allow organizations to return to previous approaches to selection and promotion, it is more probable that these requirements will be around long enough to compel continuing organizational attention. Thus it would behoove organizations to develop policies and programs that make equal opportunity a sustained effort rather than a response to immediate governmental demand. The development of a mechanism to facilitate individual, group, and organizational manpower planning is one such continuing effort.

The introduction of such a human resource planning mechanism would respond as well to other individual and organizational needs identified by this study, on at least two levels. First, when jobs undergo technological change, even change that may extend over a decade, organizations would be advised to provide planning time and resources to develop and deploy their personnel. These resources should be commensurate with the resources allotted for technological change. One of the jobs I had chosen to study was particularly vulnerable to technological change and was to be cut back over time. The threat of impending cutback created some uncertainty for employees about their future work and seemed to have contributed to negative individual feelings and work behavior, as seen in such a barometer as absences. Absences are not useful for organizations. Employees in the job vulnerable to cutback tended to be absent more than other employees. The vivid difference in absence rates is an indication of problems in the job with high rates and suggests that attention be directed toward ameliorating the situation that fosters such high absence rates. This attention could take a variety of forms but should recognize that the information about work force reduction may become known before official communications. The "handwriting on the wall" about an impending job loss may be clear to employees before the organization chooses to inform them about this cutback. Indirect information and rumor generate anxiety and concern with little or no formal opportunity for modification of these reactions. The organization might intervene by assigning a human resources staff to career development planning for all employees in vulnerable jobs, based on the company's knowledge of scheduled technological change. Individual planning could then keep pace with the introduction of technological change and subsequent work force reduction. For example, employees could be studying data processing at night for a few years before their jobs are phased out; when the cutback occurs, they will be prepared to make choices about organizational positions and options other than settling for an unskilled job. Certainly ability to predict and control actual manpower need is far from perfect, yet more accurate and supported efforts can be made.

Career development planning is important for others whose needs were identified by this study. It has been clear that future career planning is at issue for both men and women in New Type jobs. Perhaps because of the uncertainty of current promotion policies and the ambiguity of role models, the New Types' actual possibilities for upward movement in the organization may be at best uncertain; certainly they are confusing for both men and women. Such uncertainty may help to create a climate of unrealistic expectations, especially for those for whom mobility is important, namely men. It may discourage those for whom mobility has historically been less important, namely women. For both New Type males and New Type females, the addition of realistic career development planning is an appropriate organizational intervention. A career development resource for all employees could match individual risks and options with information about organizational plans and priorities. Information-based planning should be more effective for all employees than the current tradition-based arrangement, which falls short in the nontraditional work situation. Since any job is a

dead-end job if there is no place to go, all employees
should be considered potential and actual clients of such a resource, though its most immediate and primary effort is recommended for the men and women in New Type positions and all those in jobs potentially vulnerable to cutback.

Other reports support the more extensive need for a new human resources planning resource. Previous work by Rosenbaum and Schreiber based on group interviews with male and female managers found that male and female managers in the same company shared certain concerns and experiences with non-management employees, most pointedly the need for career development planning, especially among women in management.[8] These women were also New Types, as are their female nonmanagement counterparts, and they expressed far more explicit frustration about their career development. Male managers, on the other hand, are in Same Type positions, which are now less secure than they were in the past. These men reported concerns similar to those of the males in Same Type positions in this study. They, too, express frustration and confusion about future possibilities. A mechanism for personal and organizational planning could counteract some of the ambiguity and frustration by providing a sense of individual input to and control over decisions and plans about future work in the organization.

These recommendations, based on specific empirical evidence, have been confirmed and amplified in a recent article by Schein.[9] Schein recommends that organizations develop a comprehensive operation for human resource planning and development that carefully monitors the changing needs and demands of individuals and the organization and seeks the optimal match of employee need and skill with organizational development. Schein recommends that personnel specialists and line managers be involved in this function so that the operation can be integrated into the daily life of an organization on all levels. The resource would thus go beyond the remedial and become part of the organization's plan for normal growth and change.

Clearly, no matter how extensive the innovative planning effort, unpredictable environmental events will have implications beyond the vision and planning capabilities of any staff specialist or organization. No human resources effort can create certain and stable environments for organizations and employees. Still, a reliable, continuous, and involving resource would go a long way toward providing a dependable tool for decision making, useful in times of crisis or calm.

Changing Places

As Ernest Green has noted, in his preface to the fourth revised version of the *Dictionary of Occupational Titles*, in the past decade we have seen major changes in employment and unemployment in this country, reflecting "the effects of a still not fully digested mixture of unprecedented technological progress in some industrial areas, war and peacetime economic shifts, and conflicting sociological developments."[10]

This study has reflected shifts and conflicts and has had goals and outcomes similar to the Labor Department's interests in changing job names. I have sought to provide information about a phenomenon in flux in the hope that the information will be useful to employers, employees, and scholars alike and that the information itself will offer a useful tool for further policy and program development.

In the end change begets change. Technology, economy, and government stimulate organizational response, and that response pummels an organization into new and unexpected shapes. To keep organizational response to the environment sensitive and appropriate requires an internal system that can modify with some flexibility, that can itself initiate change as a result of systematic planning rather than defensive reaction. The capability for systematic planning is inherent in any organization as long as it enumerates its resources in human as well as financial and technological terms. This study sought to make a contribution to the enumerating capability of one organization and will continue to do so through systematic feedback. I hope that its findings and questions will prove beneficial to other organizations, research projects, and behavioral science theory.

EPILOGUE THE RESEARCH APPROACH: SAGA AND STRUCTURE

When I first proposed this study to my academic advisors and to the managers at BCO, I envisioned a follow-up study of the men and women who had moved into sex-atypical nonmanagement jobs in the organization. Once the company's interest in such a study was identified informally, the formal research agenda was developed. This agenda presented the extent and kind of information I would need to conduct the study I had proposed. This agenda was discussed, expanded with a contractual letter, and agreed on in a meeting with human resource managers in early 1976. One participant at this meeting was a high-level female manager who was to become the organizational liaison for the project.

Among the original resources provided by the company was a printout of all company jobs, occupancy rates, and sex composition over the past three years. This list was the basis for decisions about which jobs to include in the study. The organization had suggested an array of six jobs from which a sample group of male and female employees might be selected. Because the jobs were comparable neither in pay nor organizational level, I decided to study only two jobs; both had large enough populations of men and women to generate adequate sample sizes.

There were some major practical and theoretical drawbacks to the focus on these two jobs. That only two were large enough for study is itself a comment about the movement of men and women into jobs not considered typical for their sex. Among the practical liabilities were the disproportionate numbers of nontraditional employees in each job. For example, in 1975 women constituted 26 percent of the male-job occupants, while men constituted only 2.3 percent of the female-job occupants. This lack of comparability limited study of the effects or proportions on individual experience and outcomes.

A second drawback was that the annual statistics highlighted a three-year decline in the total number of employees in the male-type job. In 1973 there were 216 employees in the job (21 percent female); in 1974 there were 202 (26 percent female); and in 1975 there were 199 (26 percent female). The clerical (female) job displayed a similar pattern of declining numbers, but this decline was not as nettlesome because the absolute number of men in the job increased over the years.

Despite these drawbacks, there were advantages to the two-job focus. The jobs offered comparable salary ranges, required similar levels of skill development, and provided adequate numbers for sample selection. For these reasons, concerns about the actual changing composition of the jobs were brushed aside as the groundwork began.

Among the numerous tasks required by a field research project are the establishment of personal contacts, the acquisition of familiarizing information about the organization, and for this study in particular the development of a sense of the language, climate, and context of the job within the organization. All this precedes or coincides with instrument development and study implementation. Ideally the two processes of instrument development and organizational refinement cross-fertilize to make the investigation more realistic.

One by-product of a continuing contact with the organization for this investigation was the nourishment of the questions that had come up early in the project. These questions pertained to the declining population of the male job selected for the study. As they provided information about this job, personnel managers would mention changes in the section in which the job was located, such as technological innovation, and potential long-range reduction of the work force in this area. Once I became sensitive to connections among these comments, I began to wonder about the potential threat to employees in these positions, both male and female. Management generally agreed that the completion of technological innovation was not imminent, that the computer transformation of technology would not take place for twenty years. For now, these jobs were not threatened, nor would individual perceptions of future in the company be modified by threat of change in their jobs or reduction in the work force. Still, all agreed that the fact that no one had been hired for the job in a year was a sign of change.

Two months after the initial introduction, I had the opportunity to know the jobs firsthand. At this time I became fully aware of the potential and actual changes in the male job. The job's training site was virtually empty of trainers and trainees. Equipment lay unused, rooms were empty. There were no plans for future training, according to the training director. A subsequent visit to a work site brought further questions. At this work site, where there were about a dozen employees, a lengthy conversation with a supervisor confirmed my earlier suspicions. The jobs selected for study were being phased out. Although it would take many years to complete the phasing out, supervisors and employees were aware of the change and were responding with concern, according to an informant and my own observations. After this visit, it became apparent that the research purpose could be jeopardized by a changing work force. The study of stress associated with occupancy of a sex-atypical job could easily be confounded by the concurrent stress of threatened job loss for 50 percent of the proposed study sample.

At this point I decided to change the sample for study. A difficult question was whether to include this vulnerable job. There were not enough other male jobs with female occupants that were comparable to female jobs with male occupants. Also, if the job was excluded, the opportunity to study the company's "success story" would be lost. Personnel managers pointed out from the beginning that this job represented the most successful integration of men and women into a job in the company thus far.

Thus because of the problem of comparability and the lack of other possible male jobs for study, this job was included in a portion of the study that accounted for only about a quarter of the total sample of 100. Including the job allowed me to organize data analysis in such a way as to compare this job to others in the sample. About a month and a half before the study's target date, the range of jobs was expanded to eight—four male jobs and four female jobs, each having different proportions of nontraditional membership. Other sources of variability were added as the number of types and jobs included in the study expanded. But there was no alternative.

The Research Enterprise Chronicle: Commentary

Why was this lengthy report of apparently inconsequential decisions necessary? Why describe my doubts, suspicions, and uncertainties, since the decision to study eight different jobs could be reported with certainty, as a result of a rational process? My initial impulse was to present it this way, to ignore the doubt, because the presentation of doubt is embarrassing. Within the mode and format prescribed by behavioral science tradition, doubt is inadmissible evidence. Somehow we are supposed to have the prescience to know how things will turn out. When we err in our predictions, even at the earliest stages of our work, that error or misperception must be camouflaged by the cloak of certainty and rationality that is assumed to be characteristic of the scientific endeavor.

Perhaps to approximate the physical sciences, we have to come to equate scientific control with control of the research process and the research environment. Certainly such control is more possible in a laboratory setting, for both the physical and the behavioral sciences. In a field or naturalistic setting control is a scarce commodity. There are many sources of potential noncontrol in field research; so many facets of the research procedure are subject to influences beyond the control of the researcher. Sometimes these environmental elements are labeled error variance and accepted. But often they seem evidence of nonrigor in our work. As such they are to be eliminated from research reports because they are evidence of an inability to control, and thus potential evidence of our incompetence as researchers. If competence is equated with the control of variables, then incompetence is indicated by noncontrol. By reporting noncontrol, we run the risk that the report will be viewed as evidence of incompetence.

Yet messages from senior behavioral scientists exhort us to change our orientation and approach to research. Recently we have been encouraged to acknowledge the unpredicted happenings, to view them as data important to the work of science. For example, Cronbach has asserted:

An observer collecting data in one particular situation is in a position to approach a practice or proposition in that setting; observing effects in context. In trying to account for what happened, he will give attention to whatever variables were controlled, but he will give equally careful attention to *uncontrolled conditions,* to personal characterisitcs and to events that occurred during treatment and measurement. As he goes from situation to situation, his first task is to describe and interpret the effect anew in each locale, perhaps taking into account factors unique to that locale or series of events. . . . Generalizations come late and the exception is taken as seriously as the rule.[1]

Despite such compelling encouragement, it remains difficult to describe events beyond control, phenomena that are not understandable, reports that make no sense. Yet why should it be so difficult to add data to our studies, to enrich our contributions to knowledge? Perhaps because such admissions are embarrassing at first, and more profoundly, perhaps because they feel like indications of failure to make it in the research profession.

Maybe, then, it is difficult to report this evidence because we feel too strongly about it. Perhaps it becomes inadmissible because it appears to say too much about us and our abilities. Perhaps we accord it too much meaning as statements about ourselves and our limitations and allow it little value as observation about the research problem. The moments of noncontrol are taken too seriously, too personally. We believe that their significance resides in the light they cast on us and in their implications for others' evaluation of us. The belief that these moments should be kept from others thus limits an important source of information.

Heeding Cronbach's advice, I have chronicled some of the questions and uncertainties that accompanied this project as it developed. The regular logs that I kept provide information about data, its acquisition, and some of my feelings during the data gathering. These feelings often began as nagging concerns after particular conversations or interactions. More conversations and interactions helped me clarify these concerns and formulate them as questions that soon replaced the initial worries and became useful points of inquiry. These points of inquiry directed the right questions to the right people and subsequently directed some of the most productive questions in the data analysis. In this way, some initial worries became central and usable tools for research.

One critical implication of the appreciation of doubt in one's work and reports has been highlighted by those who have made distinctions between investigative and cooperative field research. Douglass[2] proposes that the researcher recognize that organizations are complex and replete with conflicting interests that prevent the full dissemination of information even between organizational members. Once the outside researcher enters the picture, organizational "secrets" may become even more important, as the organization tries to present its best face to the public (which is represented by the outsider and potentially represented by the outsider to the public). For this reason, reliance solely on cooperative (Douglass' term) research strategies, those that build on the organization's official pronouncements, inhibit the researcher's ability to obtain a thorough understanding of the organization. Essentially to counteract this limitation means raising questions about statements or behaviors or numbers that do not make sense and relying on one's personal sense of "what makes sense" to propel one's drive toward understanding the organization. One should not assume that organizations are dishonest or that they develop conspiracies of silence or deception. Rather, some organizations, like some of us, want to show their best faces to the public, and that best face may be only a profile and not a well-rounded view.

Summary: On Performances and Secrets

On the surface one might wonder about the connections between the researcher's reluctance to report doubt and uncertainty and the necessary distinction between investigative and cooperative research, beyond the recognition of their potential effects on the research process. On reflection, though, one sees that there is a more pervasive and conceptually compelling connection between these sets of phenomena, a connection that has been made quite persuasively by Goffman.[3]

Goffman views both events as performances. A research report is a performance; the researcher is presenting her best face to the public, and the impression of competence and poise represents an important social task for the professional. It signifies much about her position in a group. An organization's public behavior is also a performance; it is a set of managed impressions before an audience or audiences. The imagery of performance is particularly cogent since it often designates "front and back" regions much like front and backstage as places where different kinds of information and behavior can be displayed. Performers before an audience may portray a version of reality different from the version they portray backstage. Secrets are similarly monitored, either intentionally or unintentionally, for the audience by the performers. As Goffman notes, there are different kinds of secrets—not all are intentionally maintained—and there is discrepant information about a performance that does not come in the form of secrets but is the result of putting together "facts about almost every performance which are incompatible with the impression fostered by the performance but which have not been collected or organized into a usable form by anyone."[4]

In this research situation, facts incompatible with the performance impression raised questions. My intention in chronicling these incompatible facts and developing questions was to document the effect of raising questions and reporting the process by which insights were acquired in a research effort. Again, as Cronbach has recommended, the two scientific disciplines, experimental control and systematic correlation, answer formal questions stated in advance. Intensive local observation goes beyond discipline to an open-minded appreciation of the surprises nature drops in the investigative net.[5] By such report, I hope that the process may be generalizable to others' research endeavors. In addition, by acknowledging the human, face-saving impulses behind partial or nondisclosures by individuals, groups, and organizations, we encourage question of official pronouncements—be they organizational policy or research reports.

The preceding discussion has described a process and the problems attached to maximizing the process as a research tool. The use of the process as a research tool is consistent with Cronbach's belief about the task of the contemporary researcher:

The special task of the social scientist in each generation is to pin down the contemporary facts. Beyond that, he shares with the humanistic scholar and the artist in the effort to gain insight into contemporary relationships, and to realign the culture's view of man with present realities.[6]

Procedures

The transition from dramaturgic to methodologic may seem jarring and untimely to some, a welcome relief from speculation to others. Different aspects of the research process are valued more by some than by others just as researchers prefer different approaches, different orientations, different styles. In this presentation I have tried to respect personal preferences while acknowledging other preferences and my respect for them, emphasizing finally the importance of different aspects of the process. True to this commitment, the following discussion abides by traditional guidelines for a methods section; it describes operations, instruments, strategies, and decisions that guided the "formal" acquisition of data.

Research Design

The original plan for research was based on simple comparisons between groups. Selecting a sample of 100 employees, with 50 males and females in nontraditional jobs and 50 males and females in traditional jobs would allow comparisons between these two groups and between and among specific subgroups. When the proposal called for the comparison of male and female occupants of two jobs, the design was quite simple. Once the two-job selection problem arose, the design remained essentially unchanged but with additional variables added for analysis.

Sample Selection

While one intent of the previous narrative was to illustrate an assertion about the research process, another purpose was to introduce discussion about the selection of jobs and job occupants for study. It would have been optimal to minimize extraneous occupational influences of differences by selecting the sample from a minimal number of jobs. The preceding discussion attempted to make it clear that the two jobs originally selected for study were not comparable because of the lack of control over particular contextual features of one of the jobs.

A further recognition of organizational reality is that it was not possible to select equivalent masculine and feminine jobs for comparison in this study, because no two jobs at comparable levels in the company had enough New Type employees to constitute an adequate sample for study. To obtain a large enough sample, it was necessary to select a broad spectrum of nonmanagement jobs, eight in all, that were comparable because they were known as masculine or feminine jobs in the company and were characterized by skewed ratios of majority to minority occupants. In this selection, a further criterion was applied, in the form of a miniapproximation version of a synthetic validity approach.[7] The intent of this approach is to analyze jobs into elements common to a number of dissimilar jobs. The technique is particularly useful for selection and placement decisions because it looks for common areas of proficiency, but it can be used as well to isolate common characteristics of apparently dissimilar jobs for research purposes. My purpose was to identify clusters of job facets that would clarify the comparability of the jobs selected for inclusion in the sample. Common characteristics were designated from the job descriptions. All jobs selected were described as skilled, and all required specific training periods that combined classroom and on-the-job training. The modal training period was twelve months, with two jobs extending to eighteen months. Four of the jobs were classified as skilled clerical jobs and required specific clerical skills. The tasks assigned to these jobs included record keeping, provision of information to other parts of the organization, and customer contact. The other four jobs were technical in their requirements and tasks. Two of these jobs required regular contact with and maintenance of mechanical equipment. The other two technical jobs involved planning about the mechanical equipment.

Once the eight jobs were selected and analyzed, complete lists of all employees in these positions were requested in the spring of 1976. The jobs and their composition are presented in appendix A. From these lists and guided by the needs of the study for equal distribution of males and females within the jobs, a stratified random sample of 200 employees was originally selected. Cluster sampling techniques were then used to randomly select the 100 employees who would be asked to participate in the study. When employees from this list were unavailable because of vacations, illness, or change in job, I selected a substitute from the original list of 200 employees.

Data Collection

Organizational Arrangements

Once the 200 original names were selected, a new organizational liaison worked with me and with the directors of training within three separate branches of the organization to introduce the study to management and to arrange for the availability of potential study participants. Letters were written and contacts initiated with the managers and supervisors necessary for subsequent contact with employees. All managers and supervisors whose employees' time would potentially be requested were sent the same letter of introduction, with instructions to direct questions or concerns to either the manager in charge of training or the overall organizational liaison. Supervisors with direct employee contact were asked for cooperation in setting up interviews. They were also advised that with the permission of the employee they would be asked to fill out a questionnaire about that employee after the interview.

This mode of organization and communication, necessary in a hierarchical organization, was time-consuming in preparation but effective and efficient in operation. Of all the contacts made, only one person refused to participate in the study; eight others had to be replaced because of illness, vacation, or recent change of job. One hundred interview-questionnaire sessions[8] (see appendix B for copies), each 1½ hours long, were conducted by two interviewers during five weeks in the summer of 1976. The interviews were held in sixteen different job locations, most often in a small private place away from the employee's work position.

At the beginning of each meeting with a participant, the interviewer introduced himself or herself and explained what the study was about, abiding by the guidelines spelled out on the front of each interview. The interviewer again emphasized that participation was voluntary, that the information shared was confidential, and that results of the study would be reported to interested participants. The interviewer introduced the format and time of the interview, mentioned the questionnaire at the end of the session, and requested permission to use the tape recorder. Only one employee was uncomfortable with the tape recorder and requested that it not be used.

At the end of each interview participants were asked to complete the questionnaire, which took about forty-five minutes. They were then asked for permission to contact their supervisors. All employees granted permission for this contact.

Selection and Training of Interviewers

Because of the magnitude of the data-gathering effort and my observations during pretest interviews, I decided to use two interviewers for the study. This decision was not made casually, since a number of precautions were necessary to ensure comparable quantity and quality of work from both interviewers. Fortunately, one month before the study data collection began, I was able to engage the interest and skills of a recent Yale divinity school graduate who had extensive background in clinical interviewing and had worked in many different sectors of the community. The interviewer was interested in the research proposal and design and was available for the intense time commitment necessary.

Building on the basic interpersonal skills of the interviewer was not difficult, and much of the "training" involved collaborative work on final revisions of the interview schedule. In this way, language and wording of questions were developed jointly, providing some assurance of comparable understanding of the questions and their meanings. Similarly, both of us were involved in decisions about ways and modes of recording information on the interview forms.

Following my first pretest interviews and before the male interviewer was hired, I decided to assign the female interviewer to the female subjects and the male interviewer to the male subjects. This decision was based on the contention that people will speak more openly with similar others and that accessibility across intergroup lines may be eased by matching interviewer and intervieweee in salient characteristics. One of the limitations of this approach is its potential introduction of "interviewer effect" as a factor affecting the collection of data.

Because of the requirements of this research project—that much information, some of it sensitive and quite personal, be shared by respondents within a short time period—I decided that the match of interviewer-interviewee sex would enhance the interview's potential effectiveness. Since it would have taken a far more complex assignment and scheduling procedure to systematically remove interviewer sex effect, I adopted the matching approach with awareness of its assets and liabilities. Inter-rater reliabilities were recorded, and testified to the interviewers' consistency with regard to recording of data. This method does not provide information about interviewer sex or personality and its influence on subject's sharing of information, a most difficult problem for researchers in general.

Data Collection: Sources

In addition to the interview and questionnaires administered to sampled employees and the questionnaire sent to their supervisors, archival data was obtained from the organization about average salaries for each position over the past three years, employment, and mobility patterns. I had expected more refined and extensive archival information, especially in the area of important outcomes such as performance ratings and use of medical services, but the organization did not systematically collect and maintain this information in a centralized resource. Thus for this information we relied on records of individual employees kept by the immediate supervisor and passed on whenever the employee changed jobs.

Instruments and Measures

Employee Interview and Questionnaire.

In general, the combined use of an interview and questionnaire in behavioral science research is recommended to enhance respondent trust. The combination of personal conversation between the skilled interviewer and respondent and the creation of an atmosphere of trust, acceptance, and safety is probably a concomitant of the interview-questionnaire combination more than it is of the questionnaire alone. For obtaining information in depth unique to this research situation, the semistructured interview is an optimal tool. On the other hand, to obtain information relevant to other work about stress, it was useful to add some widely known and reliable measures usually administered in questionnaires. Thus the combination of interview and questionnaire seemed the optimal choice.

The interview contained three basic components, designed to gather evidence about questions initially proposed (see appendix B). One of the components consisted of a set of general questions addressed to all participants. The second consisted of a set of specific questions for nontraditional employees. The third contained two alternative sets of questions for traditional employees; which set was administered depended on the respondent's experience with nontraditional employees in the work setting.

Interview Order and Sequence

The sequencing of interview questions was based more on psychological than on research logical principles. General questions were addressed both in the beginning and at the end, and the most sensitive and personal questions were asked during the middle of the interview. The interview thus ended on a fairly comfortable and superficial note and ended similarly for all respondents. The differentiating questions, for New Types and Same Types were also differentially sensitive and personal and asked the nontraditional respondents more about personal feelings and exploration. Placing these questions in the middle of the interview provided maximal opportunity for trust to develop between the interviewer and respondent and also protected the vulnerability of the respondent.

General Interview Questions

Most of the interview questions directed to all participants were composed specifically for this study, with some assistance from previous work on occupational mobility[9] and general studies of work satisfaction. The questions covered three areas: (1) general employment issues, (2) affective response to the current job, and (3) job choice, work preference and the use of informational tools provided by the organization for career decisions.

Target Group Interview Questions

The interview questions specifically designed for the New Type and Same Type Groups were generally exploratory. Their format sought to combine the descriptive, probing assets of an open-ended question with the data analytic virtues of structured responses. To accomplish this end, structured response questions were interspersed with open-ended questions, probes, and requests for further information and clarification and for "feelings about———. . . ."

This general mode of question and scaled as well as open-ended response was applied to sets of questions directed to both groups of employees, although the content and orientation of these sets of questions differed. In general the questions sought to obtain different perceptions of the entry and participation of these employees in the work setting. From the combination of perceptions, I hoped to piece together a picture of the meaning of the experiences of the male and female New Types.

New Types Questions

Questions to New Types began with a brief introduction and then sought to elicit information about attitudes and concerns before taking their current position. After asking about the respondent's personal concerns or worries, the questions focused on the interpersonal climate in which the job move was made. Were there reactions from significant others that affected your move? Did you ever worry about making the right move? What were your experiences in the job? How did peers and supervisors behave in terms of attention, help, and teasing? A particularly important question, in light of the conceptual interest in the token position, was the question about extra pressure to do the job especially well, asked of all employees. These employees were then asked about current experiences in the job, whether there had been change over time, and for some overall assessment of the length of time it took to fit in with others in the work setting. Respondents were asked whether they knew of others who did not make it in the job, for some reasons why this had happened, and how they would have felt if they made it. Finally, at the end of this section, employees were asked whether they worried about "not making it in the job."

The general purpose of these questions, quite sensitive and personal in their request of the respondent, was to learn about interpersonal and personal issues that confronted the nontraditional employee in the work setting. I was interested in learning how these issues changed over time, from the period preceding entry into the job, through entry, to the present time. Relevant here was Hughes' prediction that the status contradict would remain forever "marginal" in the work setting, never quite accepted as a peer by other members of the occupational sector or work group. Was Hughes' prediction accurate for these employees, from their points of view?

Same Types Questions

In the design of the interview, it became apparent that there had to be alternative sets of questions for the traditional sample because not all the traditional employees had worked in a setting where nontraditionals were present. Some of the job settings were quite small, often occupied by only two or three workers, and here the entry of a nontraditional employee was rare. But employees in such settings would offer interesting information and perspective on the issues of our concern, since their attitudes and feelings were relatively uncontaminated by regular contact with the New Types. They thus provided a perspective on attitudes and expectations that might have greeted the earliest New Types arrivals.

The first ten questions posed to the Same Types sought an understanding of general attitudes toward the assumption of sex-atypical work positions by those in their work setting, by themselves, or by significant others. The intention was to elicit personal opinions in the context of daily life, not general attitudes about abstract issues regarding sex-typing and its meaning to individuals, but rather specific and personal reactions to movement into sex-atypical occupations and jobs.

The remaining questions to the Same Type group focused on descriptions complementary to those asked of the nontraditionals. Employees who had worked in a setting before the arrival of a nontraditional were asked about the quality of general talk—questions raised, jokes, and so forth. Subsequent questions about behavior of peers and supervisors toward the nontraditionals were replications (using same scales) or parallel to those asked of the Same Types.

The Employee Questionnaire

The employee questionnaire consisted of ten sections that reflected the composite and complex interests of the inquiry. All sections were composed of five- or seven-point items positively and negatively worded. An effort was made to maintain consistency with seven-point items, but when measures were drawn from other studies this was not possible. Only section 5 contained items that were unique to this research and matched questions from the interview. The other sections contained instruments that had proved their reliability in other stress-related research or were necessary to the study design, such as the Job Diagnostic Survey.

Stress-Related Measures

Much of the initial orientation of this study resembled the stress-related research efforts of other behavioral scientists, modified by some contentions drawn from other sources in the literature. Consistent with previous research on job-related stress,[10] I proposed that social support from supervisor and peers (and spouse, where appropriate) would be connected to affective and behavioral responses to work-related stress. I also anticipated a difference between New Type and Same Type employees in the amount of social support they would receive on the job, especially during initial occupancy of their positions.

Since the measures of social support developed by the Michigan group had proved to be both valid and reliable in stress-related research, and since no such similar measures were readily available from the literature I consulted, I used these measures of social support and asked respondents to report twice using the same set of questions. One set was directed specifically toward their first days on the job; and one set was directed toward their current work experience.

Sections 6, 7, and 8 included measures previously identified with stress-related research. Section 6 combined items from different general moods or measures of affective state, including items to measure anxiety, tension, and depression.

Section 8 was the Job Descriptive Index.[11] The reliability of this instrument for the assessment of specific satisfactions with work, pay, promotion, supervisor, and co-workers has been reported extensively in the literature. The measure was scored and recorded in accordance with the most recent instructions of its authors.

To contend with differences between the jobs, abridged versions of the Job Diagnostic Survey[12] (short form) were used.

Employee Questionnaire: Additional Measures

In addition to the measures drawn from more traditional stress-related research and general research in organizational behavior, items were invented to measure central constructs. They were repeated, in parallel form, in questions to the supervisor about the employee. The central constructs are self-perceived appropriateness of job, self-perceived job abilities, self-perceived confidence in job, self-perceived social fit in work setting, self-perceived view of future in the organization.

Supervisor Questionnaire

The supervisor's letter and questionnaire were necessarily short, and directed primarily toward record-related information, since this was the only source of such information about the employee. An additional constraint on length was the inclusion of some employees who worked under the same supervisor. Some supervisors had to complete two or three questionnaires.

Aside from record-based information about performance ratings and employee absences, the supervisors were asked about (1) their subordinates in general, (2) experiences as a subordinate with a boss of the opposite sex, (3) race and sex composition of their work group, (4) employee practices with subordinates, (5) personal demographic information, (6) work history in the organization. Supervisors were also asked to assess subordinates on the characteristics of appropriateness to job, self-confidence in job, performance in job, social fit in work setting, and future in the work organization, using the same items that had been directed to the employees. Like the employees, the supervisors were asked about general capacities of men and women for the particular job they supervised and general opportunities for men and women in the organization.

Scale Development

The scales used to test the original working hypotheses of the study were obtained from separate factor analyses of related items from the employee questionnaire, employee interview, and supervisor questionnaire, using Principal Components Analysis with varimax rotation (orthogonal). Factors with eigenvalues greater than 1.00 were retained. Items within the factors were retained when they loaded 0.50 or more on one factor and less than 0.30 on other factors. The final scales approximated the following constructs.

Employees' perceptual responses to the job: Self-perceived appropriateness to job, self-confidence in job, self-perceived potential for future mobility in company, social fit; and job future ambiguity.

Affective response to job: Job tension; somatic digestive complaints.

General affective response: General mood, vigor, tension, aggravation, general anxiety, tiredness, depression.

Social support in job, past: Supervisor support, Peer and spouse support.

Social Support in Job, present: Supervisor support, peer, spouse support.

Supervisor's perception and evaluation of employee: Job appropriateness, employee confidence, employee social fit, employee potential for future mobility in company, employee performance and abilities.

Outcomes of the factor analytic procedures guided scale composition; consequently certain items were eliminated from scale construction. Some of the originally intended employee-supervisor correspondence in scales was slightly modified for specific scales. Subsequent to the factor-analytic procedure, Spearman-Brown reliability coefficients were computed, based on the intercorrelations between items for each scale.

Interview: Descriptive Questions and Scales

The interview consisted of questions that combined structured, scaled responses with open-ended exploration; different questions were directed toward the different subgroups Because of the exploratory nature of these questions and their qualification more as descriptive and less as psychometric measures, the data elicited by these sources has not been treated by the same procedures as those used for the questionnaires. When in scale form, this data has been retained in its original form (as straightforward ordinal information) and is examined, analyzed, and interpreted as such. Thus single-item measures are deployed in the descriptive sections, and these measures are featured only in those analyses appropriate to the ordinal level of measurement used. The general format of these scales was a five-point continuum.

When open-ended questions were content-analyzed, they were not coded for this phase of the study. The material elicited by the interview is used directly from the interview sheets or the tapes as independent qualitative material or to illustrate, illuminate, or interpret quantitative material.

The Investigative Net: Warp and Woof

These two methods sections have described the procedures and perceptual tools used to generate information about the research problem. Toward this end I have described some of the organizational context as it became known through immersion in the research. All the information that shaped the design and outcome of the study came from both traditional and nontraditional sources; and much of the foresight, insight, and hindsight was provided by questions intuitively raised and responses neither scaled nor factor-analyzed— surprises caught in a capacious investigative net.

APPENDIXES

APPENDIX A

Selected Jobs: Male-Female Proportions of Occupancy 1973–1976

Job Title	1973					1974					1975					1976				
	N	M	M%	F	F%	N	M	M%	F	F%	N	M	M%	F	F%	N	M	M%	F	F%
Senior Planning Technician	211	207	98	4	2	224	220	98	4	2	216	212	98	4	2	233	223	96	10	4
Junior Planning Technician	168	153	91	15	9	166	141	85	25	15	162	137	85	25	15	151	129	85	22	15
Senior Craft Technician	827	825	99.8	2	2	813	802	98.6	11	4	795	787	99	8	1	759	752	99	7	1
Junior Craft Technician	216	170	79	46	21	202	149	74	53	26	199	148	74	51	26	173	131	76	42	24
Clerical-Service	663	2	3	661	99.7	646	28	4	618	95.6	648	46	7	602	93	638	57	9	581	91
Clerical-Support	19	0	0	19	100	21	0	0	21	100	21	2	10	19	90	22	3	14	19	86
Clerical-Support	46	0	0	46	100	48	2	4	46	96	44	2	5	42	95	43	2	5	41	95
Clerical-Support	not listed in 1973					39	2	5	37	95	47	3	6	44	94	53	4	8	49	92

APPENDIX B
RESEARCH INSTRUMENTS

VERSION #2

Carol Schreiber Research Introduction
Introduction:

Directions (to find office)

Employee: _____
     Address: _____
Super Name: _____
Super Address: _____
Job Title _____
Location _____
Date _____ Age: ____ R: ____
Interviewer _____

Circle: F   M
           T   NT

Number   _____

     My name is _____ and I am a graduate student at Yale, working on a study of men and women here   who have begun to work in clerical, craft and other non-management jobs within the past few years. I have asked for permission to talk with you today, and have arranged it through your supervisor. Even though I arranged our meeting through your supervisor I hope that you are participating in the study voluntarily -- Is that so for you?

     We will probably be talking together for about an hour, and I'll ask you questions about your work and your current life. After that I'll ask you to fill out a questionnaire which should take about a half an hour.

     Do you have any questions?

     Whatever we discuss today will be kept completely confidential and anonymous. No one here will see any of the information from this study, until it is summarized in terms of groups -- no individuals will be identified at any point in the study. I hope that knowing this will help you be frank and honest in response to these questions.

     Any questions:

     One more request -- so that I can pay attention to our conversation, it would be helpful to me if I could tape this interview, though I may also take some notes while we talk. No one but me will ever hear the tape, and it will be erased as soon as I finish with it. Is it ok with you if I use the tape recorder?

     If there is any time during our conversation that you would like me to turn the recorder off, just let me know and I will do it.

     Any more questions? If not, then let's start off by talking about your present job here...................................

1. How long have you had this job?   171

   Since: Score (# months) _____
   No. of Years

---

2. Did you have any other full-time jobs before you came here?
                                                        Yes = 1
                                                        No = 2
                 If yes, what were they?   _____
                                           _____
                                           _____
                                           _____

---

3. Was this your first full-time job here?
                                                        Yes = 1
                                                        No = 2
                 If no, what were the previous jobs?
                                                        Score: (1-15)

   _____   _____
   _____   _____
   _____   _____

---

4. Did you choose the job you have today, or were you assigned to it?
                                                        1 = Choose
                                                        2 = Assigned

---

5. Was this job a promotion, or a lateral move for you?
                                                        1 = Promotion
                                                        2 = Lateral
                                                        3 = Downgrade
                                                        4 = Administrative

---

6. Do you remember why you first took the job (Interviewer: circle
   main reason given -- only one)
                                         1 = more pay
                                         2 = promotion for itself
                                         3 = promotion as part
                                             of upward movement
                                         4 = learn new skills
                                         5 = wanted different
                                             kind of work experi-
                                             ence
                                         6 = disliked old job
                                         7 = easier work
                                         8 = work more appro-
                                             priate to me
                                         9 = other _____

---

7. How about the formal training course for this job, how much preparation
   did it give you?
   1   2   3   4   5
   Very   Some   A great deal
   Little

8. Where did you get most of your learning about the job? (Interviewer: circle all mentioned)

From			
training? = 1		6 = s+w
Supervisor = 2		7 = w+e
Other workers = 3		8 = s+e
Trial & error = 4		9 = s+t
Other = 5		10 = t+w
		11 = t+e

Now, about the job itself...

10. All in all, as of today, would you say that you liked your job?

1	2	3	4	5	6	7
Dislike very much	Dislike	Dislike Somewhat	Neutral	Like Somewhat	Like	Like very much

---

11. How appropriate do you think this job is for a person like you?

1	2	3	4	5	6	7
Very Inap.	Inap	Somewhat .Inap	Ok	Somewhat Approp	Approp	Very Approp

---

13. Have you ever felt that this might not be the right job for you?

1	2	3	4	5	6	7
Never	Rarely	Infrequently	Once or twice	Sometimes	Often	Always

14. Probe: What makes you feel that way?

(For Traditionals)

50. a) Did you ever doubt that you were making the right move, when you first took the job?

1	2	3	4	5
Never	Rarely	Sometimes	Often	Always

63. When you first started here, did you feel extra pressure to do the job especially well?

1	2	3	4	5
never	Rarely	Sometimes	Often	Always

75. Did you ever worry about not making it in this job?

1	2	3	4	5
Never	Rarely	Sometimes	Often	Always

71. Now do you feel extra pressure to do this job especially well?

1	2	3	4	5
Never	Rarely	Sometimes	Often	Always

15a. Suppose you won Grand Prize in the lottery, and had an income for life, would you continue to work at this job, shift to something else, or retire?

   b. 1 = stay in this job
   2 = shift to something else/b. What? _____
   3 = retire/b. what would you do? _____

17. What type of work would you try to get into if you could start all over
    again at anything?

18. PROBE: WHY WOULD YOU PREFER THIS TO THE WORK YOU ARE DOING NOW?

19. When you first began working here, was there a job you wanted to
    reach?   1= Yes, What was it _____
                                                      2= No   (Rank 1-15)

20. How about now, is there a job you most want to reach?
                                                      1= Yes, What is it _____
                                                      2= No (Rank 1-15)

21. What are your chances of getting this job?
    1   2   3   4   5
    Poor   Fair   All right   Pretty good Excellent

22. Have you ever actually tried to get into another line of work?
            a. Outside this company?   1=Yes _____type
                                                   2=No
            b. How about here?   1=Yes
                                                   2=No

23. Do you have any requests in now to transfer?
                                              a.   1=Yes
                                                   2=No
            b. How many?   _____
            c. For what kinds of jobs?   _____
                                                   _____
                                                   _____
                                                   _____

24. Have you talked about future job or career plans with
anyone at the company?

    a) Who? _____

4.

1 = Yes
2 = No

174

25.

26.

27. About how long would you like to work in the job you have now?
(Interviewer: Push for some specific answer = time estimate)

Record Verbatim Comments: _____

28. What do you expect to be doing after you leave this job? _____

RVC:

29. Some jobs seem to lead to many jobs and some to only a few. Does this job
give you many or few possibilities for the future?

1	2	3	4	5
None	Very limited	A few	Enough Some	Many

30. What kinds of jobs have people taken after leaving this job?
(RVC)
List:

31.a. Are any of these possibilities for you?

  b. Why or why not?

1 = Yes _____
2 = No

---

32. Sometimes people feel some worry or strain about their futures in relation to work. How about you, have you felt some worry, much worry, or no worry about your future job opportunities?

1	2	3	4	5
No worry		Some worry		A great deal of worry

---

33. Who do you think has more control over your future here , you, or the company? ---- What % of control does the Co. have? _____
                                 What % of control do you have? _____

---

34. Taking everything into account, what would you hope to be doing 5 years from now? (If finds 5 years too hard, ask, how about 1 year from now)

  a) 5 yrs.:
  b) 1 yr.:
  c) 6 months:

---

35. What do you expect to be doing five (one) years from now?

  a) 5 yrs.:
  b) 1 yr.:
  c) 6 months

If traditional, turn to q. 76, p. 11.

Introducing men and women into new kinds of jobs has been a fairly recent change here   I'm interested in talking with you about your reactions to being in a job mostly assigned in the past to men/women. (Circle one)

36. Is this the first job you've had that's not usually been done by a man/woman? (Interviewer -- circle in advance for yourself)

1 = Yes
2 = No_____

If not, what did you do previously? _____

---

37. Why do you think a man/woman would want a job like this one?

---

38. What were some of your questions or apprehensions about taking a job typically done by men/women?

---

39. Could you say more about that?

---

41. How did members of your family or your close friends react when you said you were taking this job? (Interviewer -- circle which applies in question -- could be both)

42. What were their concerns or questions? (If response was positive, ask, were their any concerns or questions? And they what were they?)

43. Did anyone try to talk you out of it?   1 = Yes
                                                  2 = No

44. If yes, what did they say?

45. a. Were you teased at all?   1 = Yes
                                                  2 = No
    b. If yes, by whom?

    c. What did they tease you about?

    d. How did you feel about it?

50. a) Did you ever doubt that you were making the right move?
    1   2   3   4   5
    Never   Rarely   Sometimes Often   Always
    b) For how long did you have these doubts?

    c) Did you talk about them with anyone?

51. How about when you first came on the job? Had there been any other men/women here before you? (Or were there at the time?)
                                    1 = Yes _____ How many
                                    2 = No

52. How would you describe the <u>behavior</u> of <u>other employees</u> toward you when
    you first took the job...Would you say that they were ACCEPTING, INDIFFERENT,
    OR REJECTING OF YOU?

1	2	3	4	5
Very Rejecting	Somewhat Rejecting	Neutral Indifferent	Somewhat Accepting	Very Accepting

53. PROBE: What were they like?

    RVC:

54. Were you <u>treated differently</u> than other new workers by the employees?

1	2	3	4	5
No Difference	Very Little	A Little	Somewhat Differently	Very Differently

    RVC:

55. Was more or less attention paid to you by co-workers than to other new employees?

1	2	3	4	5
Much Less	Somewhat Less	Same Amount	Somewhat More	Much More

    RVC:

56. Were you helped with the job more or less than others by other employees?

1	2	3	4	5
Helped Much Less	Helped Less	Same Amount	Helped More	Helped Much More

    RVC:

57. When you first started here, how much teasing was there of you by other workers?

1	2	3	4	5
Very much	Much teasing	Some	Very little	None

    RVC:

PROBE, IF 1,2,3,4

58. a. What kinds of things did they say?

b. How did you feel about that?

c. What was your reaction?

---

59. When you first took the job, was your supervisor a man or woman?

1 = same
2 = different

---

60. How would you describe your supervisor's initial treatment of you? Was he/she accepting, indifferent, or rejecting of you?

1	2	3	4	5
Very Rejecting	Somewhat Rejecting	Indifferent Neutral	Somewhat Accepting	Very Accepting

RVC:

---

61. Were you treated any differently by your supervisor than other new workers in general?

1	2	3	4	5
No Difference	Very Little	A little	Somewhat Differently	Very Differently

RVC:

---

62. Was more or less attention paid to you than to new (male/female) (traditional) employees by the supervisor?

1	2	3	4	5
Much less	Less	Same Amount	More	Much more

63. When you first started work here, did you feel extra pressure to do the job especially well?

1	2	3	4	5
Never	Rarely	Sometimes	Frequently	Always

a) Probe: Was that related to the way you were treated by co-workers or supervisors?

---

64. How about now, has there been a change in the way you are treated by your supervisor?

1	2	3	4	5
Very much change	Much change	Some-average change	Very little	None

RVC:

65. Has there been a change in the way you are treated by co-workers?

1	2	3	4	5
Very much change	Much change	Some-average change	Very little	None

RVC:

---

66. PROBE: IF TIME (COULD YOU SAY SOMETHING MORE ABOUT THAT?)

---

67. Do you think it took you any longer than other employees to feel that you fit in here?

1	2	3	4	5
Much Shorter	Shorter	Same Amount	Longer	Much Longer

RVC:

---

68. Now, when you work with other departments or with customers, how would you describe their behavior towards you? Are they accepting, indifferent, or rejecting?

1	2	3	4	5
Very Rejecting	Somewhat Rejecting	Indifferent Neutral	Somewhat Accepting	Very Accepting

RVC:

---

69. Right now, do others' behavior or comments to you effect the way you do your job?

1	2	3	4	5
Affects a lot	Affects Somewhat	A Little	Very Little	Not at all

RVC:

---

70. Right now, do the reactions or comments of other people affect your feelings?

1	2	3	4	5
Affects a lot	Somewhat	A Little	Very Little	Not at all

RVC:

71. Now, do you feel extra pressure to do the job especially well?

1	2	3	4	5
Never	Rarely	Sometimes	Frequently	Always

RVC:

If time:

72. In general, what kinds of qualities does it take for a man/woman to do this job well?

RVC:

---

73. a. Do you know any men/women who didn't stay in this job beyond six months?

                                                    1 = Yes
                                                    2 = No

    b. If yes, why didn't they(he/she) make it in the job?

    c. Can you say more about that?

---

74. (If here less than 6 months) How would you feel if you didn't make it in this job?
(More than 6 months) How would you have felt if you didn't make it in this job?

RVC:

---

75. Do(did) you worry at all about not making it here?

1	2	3	4	5
Never	Rarely	Sometimes	Often	Always

Traditionals: One of the things that's happened here over the past five years has been the introduction of men and women into jobs where they haven't been before. Since there have been some _____ moved into your job, let's talk about some of your impressions about this change.......

76. First of all, do you have any ideas about why a man/woman would want a job like this one?

77. a. How about you, would you put in a transfer for a "male" or "female"
         job? (Interviewer, circle in advance)   1 = Yes, go to Q. 78
                                                  2 = No, go to 77b

77. b. If no, ask: Would you consider it if it were higher paying than
         your present job?   1 = Yes, go to Q. 78
                             2 = No, go to 77c

77. c. If still no, then ask, are there any circumstances which would lead
         you to put in a transfer for that kind of job?
                             1 = Yes
                             2 = No
RVC:

78. What kinds of questions would you have about moving into a "man's"/
     "woman's" job?

79. PROBE: COULD YOU SAY MORE ABOUT THAT?

80. (For women) How would you feel if your husband, boyfriend or brother took
     a "woman's" job (assuming that it was better paying than the job he has at
     present)?

81. (For men) How would you feel if your wife, girlfriend, or sister took a
     "man's" job (assuming that it was better paying than her present job)?

82. (For all) What would you worry about?

84. a. Would your estimation or opinion go up/down or stay the same?

1	2	3	4	5
Way Down	Down	Stay Same	Up	Way Up

87. Have you worked in an office where there/s been a man/woman(NT)?

If no, skip to question 103 (p.15)
If yes, continue

1 = Yes
2 = No

88. Were you already working there before the first man/woman began in the job?

If no, skip to question 106 (p. 15)
If yes, continue

1 = Yes
2 = NO

89. a. What were some of the things that people talked about here when they found out that a man/woman was coming to work here?

PROBE: b. Anything you wondered about the person?

c. Were there any jokes about the person?

d. Can you give me an example of one?

90. How would you describe the behavior of other employees to this new employee when he/she first began to work here? Were people accepting, indifferent, or rejecting at first?

1	2	3	4	5
Very Rejecting	Somewhat Rejecting	Indifferent	Somewhat Accepting	Very Accepting

91. Was this person treated any differently by other employees than other workers new to the job?

1	2	3	4	5
No Difference	Very Little Difference	A Little Difference	Some Difference	Very Much Difference

92. Was more or less attention paid to this person than is usually paid to new workers here?

1	2	3	4	5
Much Less	Somewhat Less	Same Amount	Somewhat More	Much More

RVC:

---

93. Were you and others more or less helpful with the job to this person than you usually are to other new workers?

1	2	3	4	5
Helped Much Less	Somewhat Less	Same Amount	Somewhat More	Helped Much More

RVC:

---

94. In the beginning, how much teasing was there of the new person by other employees?

1	2	3	4	5
None	Hardly any	Some	A Moderate Amount	Very Much

RVC:

---

95. What about supervisors, did they give more or less attention to the new worker than to other new employees?

1	2	3	4	5
Much Less	Somewhat Less	Same Amount	Somewhat More	Much More

RVC:

---

96. Were supervisors more or less helpful to the male/female than to other employees?

1	2	3	4	5
Much Less	Somewhat Less	Same Amount	Somewhat More	Much More

---

97. In your opinion, were supervisors generally accepting, indifferent, or rejecting to the male/female?

1	2	3	4	5
Very Rejecting	Somewhat Rejecting	Indifferent	Somewhat Accepting	Very Accepting

RVC:

---

98. At first, in general, between the other workers and the supervisors do you think there was more or less attention paid to the male/female's performance on the job?

1	2	3	4	5
Much Less Attention	Somewhat Less	Same Amount	Somewhat More	Much More

RVC:

99. In general, did you sense that there was more or less pressure to do
the job well than is applied to the usual employee?

1	2	3	4	5.
Much Less Pressure	Somewhat Less Pressure	No Difference	Somewhat More Pressure	Much More Pressure

RVC:

---

100. How about now, has there been any change in the way the man/woman is treated
by other employees?

1	2	3	4	5
Very Much Change	Much	Some	Very Little	None

RVC:

---

101. Has there been a change in the way this person seems to be treated by
supervisors?

1	2	3	4	5
Very Much	Much	Some	Very Little	None

102. Do you think it took this person longer to "fit in" here than other
new employees?

1	2	3	4	5
Much Longer	Longer	Same Amount	Shorter	Much Shorter

STOP HERE - GO TO QUESTION 114 (p.17)

---

103. a. When you and other workers have talked about what it would be like to
have a male/female in this job, what kinds of things have you talked
about?

b. Any jokes?

c. What kinds of jokes?

d. Can you give me an example?

---

104. a. Have people talked about discomfort or worry about change in the
work atmosphere?   1 = Yes
                                                                2 = No
b. If yes, what have they talked about?

---

105. a. Are there any non-traditional men/women in any of the offices
you have contact with here?   1 = Yes
                                                                2 = No
b. What job are they in? _____

105. c. If yes, to 105a: Who does that job better, men or women? 1 = women
2 = men
3 = same

STOP HERE -- Go on to Question 114 (p. 17)

---

106. In general, are male/female employees treated differently than other employees by their co-workers here?

1	2	3	4	5
No Difference	Very Little Difference	A Little Difference	Some Difference	Very Much Difference

RVC:

---

107. Are male/female employees treated differently than others by supervisors?

1	2	3	4	5
No Difference	Very Little Difference	A Little Difference	Some Difference	Very Much Difference

RVC:

---

108. In general, do you think there is more or less attention paid by supervisors to the male/female worker's performance on the job?

1	2	3	4	5
Much Less Attention	Somewhat Less Attention	Same Amount	Somewhat More	Much More

RVC:

---

109. Would you say that male/female employees on this job have been generally treated with acceptance or rejection by other employees?

1	2	3	4	5
Very Rejecting	Somewhat Rejecting	Indifference	Somewhat Accepting	Very Accepting

RVC:

---

110. How about supervisors, have they treated male/female employees on this job with acceptance or rejection?

1	2	3	4	5
Very Rejecting	Somewhat Rejecting	Indifference	Somewhat Accepting	Very Accepting

RVC:

Continue....

111. What kinds of qualities does it take for a man/woman(NT) to do this job well?

---

112. a. Do you know any men/women who didn't stay in this job beyond 6 months?

    1 = Yes
    2 = No

    b. If yes, why didn't he/she make it in the job?

    c. Can you say more about that?

---

113. What is your opinion about men/women who don't make it in the job?

RVC:

FOR ALL:

114. In your opinion, what are the advantages that men have in doing this job?

---

115. What are the advantages that women have in doing this job?

---

116. What are the disadvantages that men have in doing this job?

---

117. What are the disadvantages that women have in doing this job?

118. Right now, do you think that men and women <u>have equal chances</u> for <u>all</u>
<u>jobs   here?</u>

1	2	3	4	5
Men better chance	Men somewhat better chance	Equal Chances	Women somewhat better	Women bette

---

119. a. What's your feeling about this? (No matter what is response above).

---

119. b. In what way could it affect your future here?

RVC:

---

120. Are you an active, inactive or moderately active member of the Union?

1 = Active
2 = Moderately
3 = Inactive
4 = Non-member

a. Did you initiate any grievances in your last job?

1 = Yes
2 = No

b. How about grievances in your present job?

1 = Yes
2 = No

---

121. Have you used the Company's educational benefit since you've worked
here?

1 = Yes
2 = No

If yes, for what courses? _____

_____

---

122. Speaking of education, how many years of school did you finish?
(Check off one for each person)

	Person	Father	Mother	Spouse
Some elementary school (1-7)	( )	( )	( )	( )
Completed elementary (8)	( )	( )	( )	( )
Some high school (1-3 years)	( )	( )	( )	( )
Graduated from high school	( )	( )	( )	( )
Technical school (type: _____)	( )	( )	( )	( )
Graduated from college (BA,BS)	( )	( )	( )	( )
Some grad school	( )	( )	( )	( )
Grad Degree	( )	( )	( )	( )

---

123. How about your father? How many years of school did he finish?

---

124. How about your mother? How many years of school did she finish?

125. What was the best job your father ever had?

b. _____

126. a. Did your mother work while you were growing up?   1 = Yes
                                                                  2 = No

    b. If yes, what was the best job she ever had?

c. _____

127. Has anyone in your family ever worked in this company ?   1 = Yes
                                                                     2 = No

128. Are you married?   1 = Yes   3 = Divorced
                       2 = No   4 = Widowed

129. a. Do you have any children?   1 = Yes
                                    2 = No

    b. If yes, how many? _____

    c. How old are they? _____

130. How many years of school did your spouse complete? (See up)

131. Does your spouse work?   1 = Yes
                           2 = No

132. What kind of job does he/she have?

133. If both work and have children, who cares for the children
while both you and your spouse work?

134. How many cases of absence for sickness have you had in the past year? _____

135. How about in the year before you took this job? _____

That was the last question of the interview....

If you have any questions for me, I'd like to hear them after you
fill out these questionnaires.......

Ending:

1. I'd like to repeat that what we've talked about today will be kept confidential and anonymous. I'd appreciate your not talking with anyone else in the company about our conversation, until the fall, when I've finished all the interviews -- the grapevine sometimes can work too well and could effect people's approaches to the study, if they know too much about it ahead of time.

2. Also, I wanted to let you know that I'm planning to send a short questionnaire to your supervisor -- which will ask mostly for information from your records -- I hope that's ok with you.

If you're interested in the outcomes of the study, I'd be happy to send you a short summary report sometime this fall. Would you like to receive a copy?

If so, what is your mailing address   _____

                                              _____

Interviewer comments or observations:

Interview:	Easy	Average	Difficult
Subject:	Comfortable	Average	Uncomfortable

Interviewer:	Comfortable	Average	Uncomfortable
	Fatigued	Average	Energized

Other:

Please describe your experiences when you first began your present job...

Please circle the numbers which apply in each set of questions.

When you first came on this job, how much did each of these people go out of their way to make your work life easier for you?

		not at all	very little	some what	pretty much	very much
A.	Your immediate supervisor	1	2	3	4	5
B.	Other people at work	1	2	3	4	5
C.	Your spouse (if married)	1	2	3	4	5

When you first came on this job, how easy was it to talk with each of the following people?

		not at all	very little	some what	pretty much	very much
A.	Your immediate supervisor	1	2	3	4	5
B.	Other people at work	1	2	3	4	5
C.	Your spouse (if married)	1	2	3	4	5

When you first started on this job, how much could each of these people be relied on when things get tough at work?

		not at all	very little	some what	pretty much	very much
A.	Your immediate supervisor	1	2	3	4	5
B.	Other people at work	1	2	3	4	5
C.	Your spouse (if married)	1	2	3	4	5

When you first came on this job, how much was each of the following people willing to listen to your personal problems?

		not at all	very little	some what	pretty much	very much
A.	Your immediate supervisor	1	2	3	4	5
B.	Other people at work	1	2	3	4	5
C.	Your spouse (if married)	1	2	3	4	5

When you first came on the job, how many people worked under your supervisor?

Total number: _____

How many males : _____

How many females: _____

Was your supervisor   male or   female (Circle which applies)

About how many people worked in your office then?   _____

About how many of these were male?   _____

About how many of these were females?   _____

Section Two

This part of the questionnaire asks you to describe your job, as <u>objectively</u> as you can.

Please do <u>not</u> use this part of the questionnaire to say how much you like or dislike your job. Questions about that will come later. Instead try to make your descriptions as accurate and objective as possible.

Please circle the number which is the most accurate description of your job.

1. To what extent does your job allow you to <u>form close personal relationships</u> on the job? (either co-workers or clients)

1------------2------------3------------4------------5------------6------------7

very little;	moderately; there	very much; a per-
instead the job	is some opportunity	son has lots of
allows only super-	to make close friends	chances to make
ficial contact		close friends
with other people		while working on
		the job

2. To what extent do <u>managers or co-workers</u> let you know how well you are doing on your job?

1------------2------------3------------4------------5------------6------------7

very little;	moderately; sometimes	very much, mana-
people almost	people may give me	gers or co-
never let me	"feedback", other times	workers provide
know how well	they may not	me with constant
I am doing		"feedback" about
		how well I am doing

3. To what extent does <u>doing the job itself</u> provide you with information about your work performance? That is, does the actual work itself provide clues about how well you are doing--aside from any direct "feedback" co-workers or supervisors may provide?

1------------2------------3------------4------------5------------6------------7

very little;	moderately; sometimes	very much; the
the job itself	doing the job provides	job is set up so
is set so I could	"feedback" to me; some-	that I get almost
work forever without	times it does not	constant "feedback"
finding out how well		as I work about
I am doing		how well I am
		doing

4. How much <u>autonomy</u> is there in your job? That is, to what extent does your job permit you to decide <u>on your own</u> how to go about doing the work?

1------------2------------3------------4------------5------------6------------7

very little;	moderate autonomy;	very much; the
the job gives	many things are standardized	job gives me
me almost no	and not under any control,	almost complete
personal "say"	but I can make some decisions	responsibility
about how and when	about the work	for deciding
the work is done		how and when the
		work is done

5. In general, how <u>significant or important</u> do you think your job is? That is, are the results of your work likely to significantly effect the lives or well-being of other people? (either inside or outside the company)

```
1-----------2-------------3------------4------------5-----------6-----------7
```

not very   moderately significant   highly signifi-
significant;   cant; the out-
the outcome of   come of my work
my work is <u>not</u>   can affect other
likely to have   people in very
important effects   important ways
on other people

6. To what extent is your job arranged so that you can obtain help or support from others whenever you need it?

```
1-----------2-------------3-----------4-------------5-----------6-----------7
```

very little;   moderately; I can ob-   very much; in
on my job almost   tain help from others   this job a great
no assistance   occasionally   deal of help and
can be obtained   support is avail-
from others   able to me

7. To what extent does your job require a lot of cooperative work with other people?

```
1-----------2-------------3-----------4------------5-----------6-----------7
```

very little;   moderately; some   very much; my
I almost never   cooperative work   job requires a
need to cooperate   with others is   great deal of
with others in   necessary   cooperative work
doing my job

8. To what extent does your job involve doing a <u>"whole" and identifiable</u> segment of work? That is, is the job a complete piece of work that has an obvious beginning and end? Or is it only a small <u>part</u> of the work which is finished by other people or by automatic machines?

```
1----------2-----------3 ----------4-----------5-----------6-----------7
```

My job is only a tiny   My job is a moderate-   My job involves
part of the overall   sized chunk of the work; doing the whole task
work to be done;   my own contribution can from start to finish;
the results of my   be seen in the final   the results of my
activities cannot be   outcome   activities are easily
seen in the final pro-   seen in the final
duct or service   product or service

9. How much <u>variety</u> is there in your job? That is, to what extent does the job require you to do many different things at work, using a variety of your skills and talents?

```
1----------2----------3-----------4-----------5-----------6-------------7
```

very little;   moderate variety   very much; the job
the job requires   requires me to do
me to do the same   many different things
routine things   using a number of
over and over   different skills and
again   talents

Listed below are a number of statements which could be used to describe a job.
Please indicate whether each statement is an accurate or inaccurate description
of your job.

Once again, please try to be as objective as you can in deciding how accurately
each statement describes your job--regardless of whether you like or dislike
your job.

Write a number in the blank beside each statement; based on the following scale:

How accurate is the statement in describing your job?

1	2	3	4	5	6	7
Very Inaccurate	Mostly Inaccurate	Slightly Inaccurate	Uncertain	Slightly Accurate	Mostly Accurate	Very Accurate

_____1. The job allows me to develop close friendships with co-workers on the job.

_____2. When I have problems in my job, it is generally difficult to obtain
help and support.

_____3. This job is one where a lot of other people can be affected by how
well the work gets done.

_____4. In this job, it is easy for me to try out new ideas on my co-workers.

_____5. Others (supervisors and co-workers) almost never give me any "feedback"
about how well I am doing my work.

_____6. The job denies me any chance to use my personal initiative or
judgment in carrying out my work.

_____7. The job requires me to use a number of complex or high-level skills.

_____8. The job is arranged so that I do not have the chance to do an entire
task from beginning to end.

_____9. A person on this job rarely has the chance to go out of the way to
help others at work.

_____10. The job itself is not very significant or importnat in the broader
scheme of things.

_____11. The job itself provides very few clues about whether or not I am per-
forming well.

_____12. The job provides me with the chance to completely finish the tasks
I begin.

_____13. My job gives me considerable opportunity for independence and
freedom in how I do the work.

How accurate is the statement in describing your job?

1	2	3	4	5	6	7
Very Inaccurate	Mostly Inaccurate	Slightly Inaccurate	Uncertain	Slightly Accurate	Mostly Accurate	Very Accurate

_____14. This job is arranged so that it is almost impossible for me to
develop really close relationships with people at work.

_____15. This job is set up so that I can easily turn to others whenever I
need some help.

_____16. Just doing the work required by the job provides many chances for
me to figure out how well I am doing.

_____17. The job is quite simple and repetitive.

_____18. My supervisor regularly keeps me informed on how well I am doing
my job.

Please describe your present experiences on this job.

Please circle the numbers which apply in each set of questions.

Now, how much does each of these people go out of their way to make your work life easier for your?

	not at all	very little	some what	pretty much	very much
A. Your immediate supervisor	1	2	3	4	5
B. Other people at work	1	2	3	4	5
C. Your spouse (if married)	1	2	3	4	5

Now, how easy is it to talk with each of the following people?

	not at all	very little	some what	pretty easy	very easy
A. Your immediate supervisor	1	2	3	4	5
B. Other people at work	1	2	3	4	5
C. Your spouse (if married)	1	2	3	4	5

Now how, much can each of these people be relied on when things get rough at work?

	not at all	very little	some what	pretty much	very much
A. Your immediate supervisor	1	2	3	4	5
B. Other people at work	1	2	3	4	5
C. Your spouse (if married)	1	2	3	4	5

Now, how much is ea h of the following people willing to listen to your personal problems?

	not at all	very little	some what	pretty much	very much
A. Your immediate supervisor	1	2	3	4	5
B. Other people at work	1	2	3	4	5
C. Your spouse (if married)	1	2	3	4	5

Now, how many people work under your supervisor?

Total number: _____

Of these, how many are male?   Total males: _____

How many are female?   Total females: _____

Is your supervisor   male   or   female (Circle which applies)

About how many people work in your office?   _____

About how many are male?   _____

About how many are female?   _____

Section Five

Each of the statements below is something that a person might say about his or her job or their future in the company. Please indicate your own personal feelings about these statements by marking how much you agree with each one.

Write a number for each statement in the blank, based on this scale:

How much do you agree with the statement?

1	2	3	4	5	6	7
Disagree Strongly	Disagree	Disagree Slightly	Neutral	Agree Slightly	Agree	Agree Strongly

____1. I am generally satisfied with the kind of work I do in this job.

____2. I am certain about what my job responsibilities will be 6 months from now.

____3. This job is very appropriate for a person like me.

____4. I have very little confidence about my general abilities.

____5. I frequently think of quitting this job.

____6. My own feelings generally are not affected much one way or the other by how well I perform.

____7. I am not accepted by co-workers.

____8. I have the ability to do more challenging work here.

____9. I have very few well-developed work skills.

____10. It bothers me to discover that I have performed poorly on this job.

____11. I am certain about what my future career picture looks like.

____12. My work on this job is not a very central part of my life.

____13. This job may not be the right one for me.

____14. My performance on the job could be improved considerably.

____15. Generally speaking, I am very satisfied with my job.

____16. My job has little relationship to the work I eventually plan to do.

____17. The major satisfaction in my life comes from my job.

____18. I feel like I "fit in" well with others on this job.

____19. I lack the potential to move up here.

____20. I have the right kind of abilities to do the job well.

____21. I am certain that my job skills will be of use five years from now.

____22. I am unsure of myself in this job.

____23. There is a good "match" between me and the requirements of this job.

____24. This job is a central part of my future work plans.

____25. In relation to this job, I am very self-confident.

____26. My opinion of myself goes up when I do this job well.

____27. Most things in life are more important than work.

____28. I feel a great sense of personal satisfaction when I do this job well.

____29. I do this job very well.

When you think about your life in general these days, <u>how much of the time do you feel this way?</u>

Write a number in the blank for each statement, based on this scale:

```
1----------2----------3-----------4------------5
```

Never	A little of the time	Some of the time	A good part of the time	Most of the time

____1.   I feel lively.   ____34.   I am efficient.

____2.   I feel nervous.   ____35.   I can't take a regular rest period each day.

____3.   I feel sad.

____4.   I feel energetic.   ____36.   I can't get regular daily exercise.

____5.   I feel jittery.   ____37.   I smoke more than 20 cigarettes a day.

____6.   I feel useful and needed. ____38.   I drink more than 6 cups of coffee a day.

____7.   I feel worn out.

____8.   I feel calm.   ____39.   I take two or more alcoholic drinks a day.

____9.   I feel restless.

____10.   I feel unhappy.

____11.   I feel alert.

____12.   I feel confused.

____13.   I feel tense.

____14.   I feel frustrated.

____15.   I feel full of pep.

____16.   I feel lonesome.

____17.   I feel good.

____18.   I feel bushed.

____19.   I feel depressed.

____20.   I get angry.

____21.   I feel relaxed.

____22.   I feel tired for no reason.

____23.   I feel anxious.

____24.   I feel fidgety.

____25.   I feel blue.

____26.   I feel carefree.

____27.   I get aggravated.

____28.   I feel wornout.

____29.   I feel cheerful.

____30.   I get irritated or annoyed.

____31.   I feel on edge.

____32.   I feel vigorous.

____33.   I feel discouraged.

Many people experience some strain or ill health as a result of working
hard at their jobs. The following questions ask about this.

Read each statement and indicate the extent to which it applies to you, using
the scale below. Place the number code of your response next to each statement in the blank on the left.

Applies to me   Applies to me
very little or   1   2   3   4   5 very much
not at all

___1. I do not have very good health.

___2. I feel restless and uneasy more often than I probably should.

___3. I am often bothered by acid indigestion or heartburn.

___4. I sometimes feel weak all over.

___5. I wake up with stiffness or aching in joints or muscles.

___6. My job tends to directly affect my health.

___7. I work under a great deal of tension.

___8. I have had trouble getting to sleep or staying asleep.

___9. I have felt fidgety or nervous as a result of my job.

__10. I have an ulcer condition.

__11. I get irritated or annoyed over the way things are going.

__12. I have fairly frequent headaches.

__13. If I had a different job, my health would probably improve.

__14. I seem to tire quickly.

__15. Job worries sometimes get me down physically.

__16. I have felt down and out fairly often.

__17. I breathe a sigh of relief when I miss a day of work.

__18. Problems associated with my job have kept me awake at night.

__19. I have worried, after making a decision, whether I did the right thing.

__20. I may now have an ulcer, but I am not sure of it.

__21. I have felt nervous before attending meetings in this organization.

__22. I often "take my job home with me" in the sense that I think about
       it when doing other things.

__23. I have trouble with my indigestion.

__24. I find I am inclined "to take things hard."

__25. I often wonder whether it's all worth it.

Please put a Y beside an item which describes your job.

Please put an N beside an item which doesn't describe your job.

Please put a ? if you can't decide.

WORK	SUPERVISION	CO-WORKERS
_____Fascinating	_____Asks my advice	_____Stimulating
_____Routine	_____Hard to please	_____Boring
_____Satisfying	_____Impolite	_____Slow
_____Boring	_____Praises good work	_____Ambitious
_____Good	_____Tactful	_____Stupid
_____Creative	_____Influential	_____Responsible
_____Respected	_____Up-to-date	_____Fast
_____Hot	_____Doesn't supervise enough	_____Intelligent
_____Pleasant	_____Quick-tempered	_____Easy to make enemies
_____Useful	_____Tells me where I stand	_____Talk too much
_____Tiresome	_____Annoying	_____Smart
_____Healthful	_____Stubborn	_____Lazy
_____Challenging	_____Knows job well	_____Unpleasant
_____On your feet	_____Bad	_____No privacy
_____Frustrating	_____Intelligent	_____Active
_____Simple	_____Leaves me on my own	_____Narrow interests
_____Endless	_____Lazy	_____Loyal
_____Gives sense of accomplishment	_____Around when needed	_____Hard to meet

PAY	PROMOTIONS
_____Income adequate for normal expenses	_____Good opportunity for advancement
_____Satisfactory fringe benefits	_____Opportunity somewhat limited
_____Barely live on income	_____Promotion on ability
_____Bad	_____Dead-end job
_____Income provides luxuries	_____Good chance for promotion
_____Insecure	_____Unfair promotion policy
_____Less than I deserve	_____Infrequent promotions
_____Highly paid	_____Regular promotions
_____Underpaid	_____Fairly good chance for promotion

Please use the following scales to indicate your reactions to the interview
and questionnaire you have just completed. Please circle the number which
most closely describes your response to the question.

1. The <u>overall feeling</u> I had about the interview just completed was:

1	2	3	4	5
Very Negative	Mildly Negative	Neutral	Mildly Positive	Very Postive

2. The extent to which I <u>felt comfortable</u> to express my opinions <u>without fear</u>.

1	2	3	4	5
Very Uncomfortable	Mildly	Neutral	Mildly	Very Comfortable

3. The <u>degree of trust</u> I had in the researchers to keep the promise of
   confidentiality.

1	2	3	4	5
Very Mistrustful	Somewhat Mistrustful	Neutral	Somewhat Trustful	Very Trustful

Yale University   *New Haven, Connecticut 06520*

SCHOOL OF ORGANIZATION AND MANAGEMENT

3742 Yale Station (56 Hillhouse Avenue)

Summer, 1976

Dear Supervisor:

This questionnaire is part of a Yale University study of men and women in
clerical, craft and other non-management jobs here. With the permission
of the company, I have randomly selected 100 employees in particular jobs
here, and have asked them to participate. One of your subordinates,
_____, has been interviewed as part of the study.
I sould appreciate your participation as well.

I am interested in two kinds of information. One is about your views of
the job you supervise and your views of this subordinate's comfort in that
job. There are also questions about your background and opinions. Both
kinds of information will make the study complete.

No participant in the study will be identified or evaluated. Your individual
answers will be kept completely confidential. Please answer each question
as honestly and frankly as possible. It is important that you leave no
questions out.

It should take about a half hour to complete these questions. When you
have finished, please use the enclosed addressed envelope to return
mail within the next week. It is important that I hear from you as soon
as possible.

Once the study is complete, I will send a brief summary feedback report
to interested participants. If you are interested, please indicate so
by addressing the enclosed envelope to yourself, and return with your
completed questionnaire.

I appreciate your taking the time to help the study. I hope that our
results will, in turn, help employees and managers.

If you have any further questions about the study, please contact your
departmental coordinator.

I look forward to hearing from you. Thank you very much.

Sincerely yours,

Carol T. Schreiber
Graduate student
Yale University School of
Organization and Management

Job Title _____

Employee's
Name _____

Section I

1. How was this employee rated on job related qualifications at first?
   Please check one.

   ___ Qualified
   ___ Qualified with additional factors
   ___ Not qualified
   ___ Did not come through Transfer Bureau

2. What was the 6 months performance evaluation of this employee?

3. Has this employee's performance been evaluated since that time?
   Please note date and rating.

   1. _____
   2. _____
   3. _____
   4. _____

4. On how many separate occasions has this employee been absent during
   the past year?
   _____

5. On how many separate occasions was this employee absent during the
   year prior to this job?
   _____

6. Has this employee initiated any grievances since taking this job?
   Please check.
   Yes ___   Number _____   Content _____
   No ___

7. How about previous jobs. Were any grievances initiated?
   Yes ___
   No ___

8. Have you spoken with this employee about other job opportunities here?
   ____ Yes. If yes, what have you discussed?

   ____ No

   \#_____

9. Do you use the job vacancy report to discuss job opportunities with employees <u>in general</u>?

    ____ Yes

    ____ No

10. During the past year, how many of your subordinates have left this job?

    Of these, how many were promotions?   _____

     _____

     _____

     _____

    Other   _____

11. How many employees do you supervise?   _____

    How many of these are female?   _____

    How many of these are male?   _____

    How many of these are the same race as you are?   _____

    How many are of a different race?   _____

12. Right now, do you report to a male or a female boss?

    Report to a female boss   _____

    Report to a male boss   _____

13. During all your years here   how many times have you reported to a male boss? How often to a female boss?

              Reported _____ times to a male boss

              Reported _____ times to a female boss

#_____

Each of the statements below is something that a supervisor might observe about an employee and the job. Please indicate your own impressions about these observations, as they apply to <u>this employee</u>, by marking how much you agree with each statement.

Write a number for each statement in the blank, based on this scale.

How much do you agree with the statement?

1 Disagree Strongly	2 Disagree	3 Disagree Slightly	4 Neutral	5 Agree Slightly	6 Agree	7 Agree Strongly

_____ 1. This job is very appropriate for a person like this employee.

_____ 2. This employee has little confidence about general abilities.

_____ 3. This employee seems to "fit in" well with others on the job.

_____ 4. The present job may not be the right one for this employee.

_____ 5. This employee has very few well-developed work skills.

_____ 6. In relation to this job, this employee is very self-confident.

_____ 7. This employee's performance on the job could be improved considerably.

_____ 8. This employee has the right kinds of abilities to do this job well.

_____ 9. This employee is not accepted by co-workers.

_____10. This employee has the ability to do more challenging work here.

_____11. This employee seems unsure in this job.

_____12. This employee does <u>this</u> job very well.

_____13. This employee lacks the potential to move up here.

_____14. There is a good "match" between this employee and the requirements of the job.

#_____

The following are some general questions about the job you supervise:

15.   In your opinion, what are the advantages that men have in doing this job?

16.   What are the advantages that women have in doing this job?

17.   What are the disadvantages that men have in doing this job?

18.   What are the disadvantages that women have in doing this job?

19. Right now, do men and women have equal chances for all jobs here?
(Circle the number which represents your opinion)

1	2	3	4	5	6	7
Men have much bet- ter chance	Men have better chance	Men have somewhat better chance	Equal Chance	Women somewhat better chance	Women have better chance	Women much better chance

Comments:

#_____

Section Three

This part of the questionnaire asks first for information about yourself. Section 4 asks about some general attitudes.

20. What is your age? _____

21. Sex: (Please circle)   Male   Female

22. Race: _____

23. Marital Status: (Please circle) Single   Married   Divorced   Separated
                                              Widowed

24. Do you have any children? _____ How many? _____   Ages _____

25. For how many years have you worked here?   _____

26. Have you ever worked in the job you supervise?_____
                          For how long?   _____
                          How many years ago? _____

27. How many years of school did you complete? _____
                     What type of school?   _____

28. Have you used the educational benefit? (Please circle)
                     Yes: How often? _____   No
                     For what kinds of courses: _____

#_____

APPENDIX C

Means and Standard Deviations: New Types and Same Types

Dimensions	Same Types (N = 50)		New Types (N = 50)		Differences (d.f. = 98)	
	$\bar{x}$	s.d.	$\bar{x}$	s.d.	t	$p < 0.10$
A. *Self-View* (7-point scale)						
1. Appropriate	4.28	1.63	4.82	1.53	1.67	0.09
2. Confidence	6.09	0.67	5.88	0.88	1.35	ns
3. Organizational Future	6.16	0.89	5.89	1.17	1.29	ns
4. Social Fit	6.02	0.85	6.05	0.83	0.18	ns
5. Job Future	3.86	1.6	4.56	1.5	2.22	0.03
B. *Supervisor View* (7-point scale)						
1. Appropriate	4.26	1.84	4.35	1.65	0.27	ns
2. Confidence	5.68	1.26	5.10	1.53	2.09	0.04
3. Organizational Future	5.09	1.74	4.98	1.47	0.34	ns
4. Social Fit	5.69	1.82	5.72	1.43	0.09	ns
5. Performance	5.14	1.26	4.78	1.48	1.33	ns
C. *Social Support* (5-point scale)						
1. Past Supervisor	3.44	0.93	3.65	1.2	0.98	ns
2. Past Peers	4.09	0.78	3.84	0.84	1.56	ns
3. Now Supervisor	3.61	0.96	3.83	0.93	1.15	ns
4. Now Peers	3.87	0.67	3.78	0.89	0.57	ns
D. *Job Characteristics* Motivating Potential Score of Job	125.0	61.9	134.3	73.3	0.68	ns
E. *JDI Satisfaction* (1–54)						
1. JDI Work	28.3	12.0	34.5	11.9	2.57	0.01
2. JDI Supervisor	39.6	12.3	42.1	11.75	1.06	ns
3. JDI Co-workers	43.6	11.5	42.3	9.9	0.61	ns
4. JDI Pay	45.0	8.3	42.7	11.9	1.14	ns
5. JDI Promotion	23.47	16.6	28.95	16.3	1.70	ns
F. *Affect Now* (5-point scale)						
1. Job Tension	1.93	0.92	1.81	0.91	0.67	ns
2. Somatic GI (stomach problems)	1.25	0.51	1.45	0.72	1.56	ns

3. Aggravation, Irritability	2.54	0.54	2.33	0.62	1.75	ns
4. General Anxiety	1.88	0.57	2.02	0.82	0.98	ns
5. Tiredness	2.10	0.63	2.13	0.75	0.22	ns
6. Depression	1.97	0.56	2.01	0.65	0.33	ns
G. *Extra Pressure* (7-point scale)	1.92	1.05	3.18	1.62	21.2	0.000

ns = not significant

p < .10 = statistically significant. When the difference between two group means is greater than we would expect to find by chance, the difference is statistically significant and the groups are significantly different on the measured characteristic. The lower the p (probability) value, the larger the difference between groups; thus low *p* values indicate a more significant difference.

APPENDIX D

Regression Model: Work Satisfaction

Variable	b	s.e.(b)	Beta	F
Length of Time in Job (months)	−0.202	0.2186	−0.345	0.858
Sex Congruence or Incongruence	7.64	9.99	0.312	0.584
Social Support, Peers	−0.47	2.12	−0.02	0.049
Social Support, Supervisor	8.68	2.25	0.355	14.77
Sex Match, Employee/Supervisor	−6.75	3.47	−0.24	3.78
Job Type 1	−17.57	9.04	−0.697	3.78
Job Type 2	−11.33	11.75	−0.30	0.92
Job Type 3	−32.72	12.33	−1.14	7.04
Job Type 4	−19.51	18.14	−0.43	1.15
Job Type 5	−4.38	10.01	−0.12	0.19
Interaction of Job Type 1, Sex Match	5.48	9.19	0.176	0.356
Interaction of Job Type 2, Sex Match	−1.63	12.31	−0.03	0.018
Interaction of Job Type 3, Sex Match	9.58	10.25	0.25	0.870
Interaction of Job Type 4, Sex Match	6.25	12.26	0.10	0.260
Interaction of Job Type 5, Sex Match	−4.06	10.29	−0.07	0.155
Interaction of Sex Match, Length of Time on Job	−0.011	0.135	−0.015	0.008
Interaction of Job Type 1, Length of Time on Job	0.224	0.224	0.298	1.005
Interaction of Job Type 2, Length of Time on Job	0.355	0.274	0.322	1.68
Interaction of Job Type 3, Length of Time on Job	0.346	0.249	0.637	1.93
Interaction of Job Type 4, Length of Time on Job	0.523	0.429	0.416	1.49
Interaction of Job Type 5, Length of Time on Job	0.333	0.251	0.292	1.76

Constant 39.09

APPENDIX E
ADDITIONAL REGRESSION ANALYSES

Regression analyses were done on other variables such as self-perceived performance, self-perceived appropriateness of the job, social support from supervisors, depression, and employee and supervisor expectation of employee future in the organization. Inclusion of this set of outcome measures represents the *affective* (social support from supervisor, depression, satisfaction with promotion) and *perceptual* (self-perceived performance and self-perceived appropriateness of the job) outcomes of interest.

Depression

In the initial designation of outcome variables common to stress research, depression was identified as a negative mood state frequently connected with stress conditions. Depression was one of a number of mood states identified and measured in the study including general anxiety, job tension, somatic gastrointestinal complaints, and psychological complaints. Depression was selected for regression analysis because of its conceptual connection with helplessness, a condition associated with environmental threat, and because in the group comparisons it reflected differences between groups, unlike the other measures of mood state.

In the analysis of depression, the twenty variables that made up the full equation accounted for an R^2 of 0.31 and an $\bar{R}^2$ of 0.16. The final equation included

Table E.1
Depression: Final Model

Variable	b	s.e.(b)	Beta	F	Usefulness
Social support from supervisor	−0.30	0.12	−0.29	7.36	0.06
New Type in junior craft	0.49	0.17	0.26	8.36	0.06
Length of Time in Clerical Job	−0.01	0.01	−0.18	3.19	0.03

Constant 2.13

three variables and accounted for an R^2 of 0.19 and an $\bar{R}^2$ of 0.16 (table E.1).

The three variables in the final model indicate that employees who report less social support from their supervisors report more depression, a finding that may have been influenced by common method variance. The New Type occupants of the junior crafts job (females) are more likely to express depression than other occupants of the job and all other employees in the study sample. Sex-atypical occupancy of the junior craft job is the only characteristic identified in the analysis that is positively associated with depression. The only other work characteristic to have survived this regression procedure is the length of time in the clerical-support positions. The newer that employees are to these jobs, the more depression they report.

Despite the interest in the b values and the support they offer to previous findings about the effect of occupancy of the junior craft job, none of the characteristics identified by the final regression analysis makes a strong contribution to our understanding of depression, as indicated by the minimal values of the usefulness statistics. In this group of variables the most potent source of information about the dependent variable comes from our knowledge of nontraditional occupancy of the junior craft job, which is consonant with the findings of previous analyses. With as much as we know about the effect of the junior craft job on negative affective outcomes, our equation does not tell us as much about depression as we have known about other dependent variables (just about 20 percent of the variation in depression is accounted for by this group of variables). Only two of the variables make important contributions to our knowledge of depression: social support from the supervisor and sex-atypical occupancy of the junior craft job.

Social Support from Supervisor

In previous analyses social support from supervisor has been treated as an independent variable and

evaluated for its contribution to the designated outcome measures. In this analysis social support was
treated as an outcome variable so that I could learn
more about the organizational, situational, and personal characteristics that contribute to this affective-
perceptual response. Social support was defined
conceptually and operationally in the same form as
previous stress research, where the presence of social support was found to enhance person-job fit and
to mediate the impact of certain stressors. In the current analyses we predicted that sex-atypical employees, especially those not of the same sex as their
supervisor, would be likely to report less positively
about social support from their supervisors. It was thus
predicted that these characteristics would be most important in determining variation in social support as
reported by employees.

The regression analysis began with the full complement of eighteen variables, which accounted for
an R^2 of 0.26 and an $\bar{R}^2$ of 0.08. The final equation,
including five variables, accounted for an R^2 of 0.20
and an $\bar{R}^2$ of 0.16. The variables are shown in table
E.2.

Table E.2
Social Support from Supervisor: Final Model

Variable	b	s.e.(b)	Beta	F	Usefulness
Sex-atypical Job Occupancy	0.50	0.19	0.26	6.66	0.06
Junior Craft Job	−1.62	0.55	−0.74	8.72	0.07
Senior Craft Job	−0.76	0.33	−0.22	5.43	0.05
New Types in Clerical Support	−1.26	0.42	−0.29	9.07	0.08
Length of Time in Junior Craft	0.02	0.01	0.49	3.90	0.03

Constant 3.76

Interpretations of the *b* values indicate that, contrary to predictions, all New Types report more positive social support in general than do Same Type employees; in other words being in a New Type position leads to a prediction of a more positive report of social support from the supervisor. Those who tend to report less social support from their supervisors are occupants of the junior craft job, occupants of the senior craft job, and finally the New Type occupants of the clerical-support jobs (males). Membership in each of these categories detracts to a greater or lesser extent from the employee's report of supervisor support. These negative effects are stronger than the positive effect exerted by New Type job occupancy and the other identified characteristic, length of time in the junior craft job. The longer occupants of the junior craft job have been in the job, the more social support from the supervisor they report, although their reports still compare unfavorably to occupants of other jobs. Again occupancy of the junior crafts job detracts from an affective resource acknowledged to mitigate the effect of stress.

Most of what we know about social support from supervisors comes from knowledge about one clerical and two crafts jobs, combined with information about New Type job occupancy. Each of these characteristics contributes a similar proportion of what is known about supervisory social support. Without knowledge about the specific jobs, the explanatory power of this equation would be undermined. Had we relied solely on univariate analyses, we would have known only about 30 percent of what we know (0.20) about variation in social support. Again the clearest contributions to our knowledge come from information about the individual job situations.

Self-Perceived Fit with Job and Self-Perceived Performance

Initially theories of social comparison led to predictions of more negative self-perceptions and self-

evaluations among the sex-atypical employees.
These perceptual responses, especially as they affect
self-view in the job, are important as sequellae attached to occupancy of sex-atypical jobs. Table E.3
highlights the results of regression analysis of self-
evaluated performance.

This combination of five variables accounted for an
R^2 of 0.23 and an $\bar{R}^2$ of 0.18, as opposed to an R^2 of
0.38 and an $\bar{R}^2$ of 0.21 for the full twenty variable
model.

Regression analyses confirm predictions about an
important relationship between sex-atypical job occupancy and self-evaluation of performance. Sex-
atypical job occupants evaluate themselves lower in
work performance, on the whole, than do the typical
job occupants, in all jobs. Occupancy of the sex-atypical position is also the most important or "useful"
information we can apply to the prediction of self
performance evaluation. Still, the final equation does
tell us that occupancy of a sex-atypical job for a longer
time counteracts the effects of sex-atypical job occu-

Table E.3
Self-Performance Evaluation: Final Model

Variable	b	s.e.(b)	Beta	F	Usefulness
Sex-Atypical Job Occupancy	1.78	0.44	−0.78	16.3	0.13
Social Support from Supervisor	0.53	0.22	0.23	5.76	0.05
Length of Time in Sex-atypical Job	0.04	0.01	0.52	12.05	0.10
New Type in Clerical-Support Job	1.11	0.56	0.21	3.84	0.03
Length of Time in Junior Craft Job	0.01	0.00	0.19	3.70	0.03

Constant 5.01

pancy on self-evaluation. In other words, time does help the sex-atypical employee in self-evaluation, though that self-evaluation continues to be affected negatively by occupancy of the sex-atypical position.

Appropriateness of the Job

Self-perceived appropriateness of the job was the other important self-percept variable about which predictions had been made from social comparison theory. We had expected to find that the sex-atypical employees would view themselves as less appropriate to their jobs due to their lack of similarity to the modal employees in the job. In the initial T-test, the sex-typical and sex-atypical groups did differ slightly on this characteristic, but a more sophisticated analysis was necessary to determine the actual components of this difference. Regression analysis with the full complement of variables accounted for an R^2 of 0.37 and an $\bar{R}^2$ of 0.19. The procedure eliminated fifteen variables, and in the final equation the five surviving characteristics accounted for an R^2 of 0.27 and an $\bar{R}^2$ of 0.23. The specific values of each variable are displayed in table E.4.

This analysis clarifies to some extent the results of the initial univariate comparisons. Clearly the most significant component of appropriateness is occu-

Table E.4

Appropriateness of Job: Final Model

Variable	b	s.e. (b)	Beta	F	Usefulness
Social Support from Supervisor	0.75	0.30	0.29	6.01	0.05
Clerical-Service Job	−0.90	0.36	−0.27	6.05	0.05
Clerical-Support Job	1.24	0.51	−0.24	5.84	0.05
Nontraditional Employees in the Junior Craft Job	1.86	0.58	0.38	10.3	0.08

Constant 4.98

pancy of the junior craft job, a condition that detracts from a positive sense of fit or match with the job. Yet the New Types in this job (females) view themselves as more appropriate to the job than do their male peers. This situation parallels that demonstrated in relation to work satisfaction, with which the concept of fit or appropriateness may in fact converge. Conceptually separate, despite their operational convergence, these two work characteristics may share the same kind of positive or negative affect generated by a work situation. In other words, a difficult work situation can have an impact both on work satisfaction and on a sense of match with the job. This self-percept may pertain more to the nature of the work situation than to the match or non-match of person-sex to job sex, contrary to my original prediction. In at least one distressing work situation, the non-match of person and job in terms of sex seems to have had a positive effect on self-perception of match with the job. The more positive feelings of job appropriateness expressed by women in the junior craft job offset the negative feelings about appropriateness generally expressed by employees in this position.

Organizational Mobility: Self and Supervisor View

As the last pair of findings generated by regression analysis, we consider two separate but related facets of the original design. I had proposed that New Type employees would have less positive feelings about their organizational future than their traditional counterparts due to the absence of similar sex role models in each job category and in management. It was also proposed that supervisors would view the New Type employees as having less potential for organizational mobility than the Same Type employees. Since the specific measures used in this situation were the same, and both supervisors and employees responded to the same items, the two sets of perceptions (expectations) are comparable analytically.

As table E.5 illustrates, among employees, with the

outcome measure of self-perceived future in the organization, the full complement of twenty variables accounted for an R^2 of 0.25 and an $\bar{R}^2$ of 0.06. The final model, which included three organizational variables, presented an R^2 of 0.16 and an $\bar{R}^2$ of 0.13. Although these values are not particularly strong compared to other R^2 generated by the study, these results are important to understanding the specific work situation under observation.

The employees with the least positive view of their potential for vertical mobility in the organization are the New Types in the junior craft job, the females. In fact, without knowing this characteristic, we would know very little about variation in the expectation among employees. Still, females in two of the other male job categories are also pessimistic about their futures in the organization, although to a lesser extent than the junior craft women. In sum, three of four groups of women in traditionally male jobs are pessimistic about upward mobility in the organization. The prediction about differences between sex-typical and sex-atypical employees in this respect applies only to the female portion of the sample and most dramatically to women in the junior craft job.

The initial combination of variables used to explain the supervisor's view of the employee's future in the organization was the same basic set of twenty, which

Table E.5

Self-View of Mobility in the Organization: Final Model

Variable	b	s.e. (b)	Beta	F	Usefulness
New Types in Junior Craft Job	−1.25	0.33	−0.39	14.2	0.13
New Types in Senior Craft Job	−0.79	0.51	−0.15	4.40	0.04
New Types in Senior Technician Job	−0.66	0.42	−0.15	2.50	0.02

Constant 6.16

accounted for an R^2 of 0.26 and an $\bar{R}^2$ of 0.06. The final
combination of five characteristics accounted for an R^2 of 0.20 and an $\bar{R}^2$ of 0.16, as presented in table E.6.

In the junior craft job, there is a major correspondence between supervisors' and the New Type female employees' views about a future in the organization. The women in the job are pessimistic about future vertical mobility, and their supervisors (all male) share this view. Other groups viewed as having less potential for vertical mobility in the organization are the occupants of the clerical-service job, a job sex-typed as female, although those who have been on the job longer seem to elicit more optimistic predictions from their supervisors. There is some association evident in this analysis between perceived social support from the supervisor and supervisor's expectation about the employee future. For employees who report more social support from their supervisors, the supervisors report more positive expectation about the employees' future.

Table E.6
Supervisor's View of Employee Mobility in the Organization: Final Model

Variable	b	s.e. (b)	Beta	F	Usefulness
Social Support from Supervisor	0.54	0.25	0.29	3.5	0.03
Clerical-Service Job	1.49	0.44	0.44	11.3	0.10
New Types in Junior Craft Job	1.75	0.44	0.44	15.5	0.13
Length of Time in Clerical Service Job	0.03	0.01	0.01	6.01	0 05

Constant 5.47

APPENDIX F

Male-Female Work Force Moves by New Type–Same Type Job Occupants

		Type of Move									
	Total	Up (Promotion)		Down		Out (Left Company)		Side (Lateral, Different Job)		Retired or Died	
		#	%	#	%	#	%	#	%	#	%
1974											
Male NT	9	0	0	1	11	8	89	0	0	0	0
Male ST	142	78	51	10	7	25	16	23	15	6	4
Female ST	102	57	56	19	19	21	20	3	3	2	2
Female NT	32	10	31	9	29	11	34	2	6	0	0
Total	285	145		39		65		28		8	
1975											
Male NT	10	4	40	3	30	3	30	0	0	0	0
Male ST	104	27	26	10	10	32	30	25	47	10	10
Female ST	102	21	21	23	22	40	39	11	11	7	7
Female NT	11	0	0	5	46	4	36	1	9	1	9
Total	227	52		41		79		37		18	
1976											
Male NT	15	7	47	6	40	2	13	0	0	0	0
Male ST	138	102	74	14	10	6	4	12	9	4	3
Female ST	127	38	30	12	9	71	56	4	3	0	0
Female NT	22	9	41	8	36	4	18	1	5	2	2
Total	302	156		40		83		17		6	

NOTES TO CHAPTER 1

1
These titles were extrapolated from the U.S. Department of Labor, *Dictionary of Occupational Titles,* Washington, D.C., 1965, 3rd rev. ed., and U.S. Department of Labor, *Dictionary of Occupational Titles,* Washington, D.C., 1974, 4th rev. ed.

2
Ernest Green, Prefatory Remarks in U.S. Department of Labor, *Dictionary of Occupational Titles,* 4th rev. ed., p. v.

3
Ibid.

4
The acts include Civil Rights Act of 1964, Title VII; Executive Order 11246, amended by Executive Order 11375, 1967; Revised Order No. 4, 1974; Executive Order 11478, 1969; Equal Employment Opportunity Commission, Revised Guidelines on Discrimination because of Sex.

5
In June 1978 the *New York Times* announced that the U.S. Government, Equal Employment Opportunity Commission, and the General Electric Company agreed to a $32 million settlement and a promise to promote women and men in response to a 1973 discrimination charge brought against the company. Included in the agreement were the provision of retroactive wage rates to female factory workers and specific efforts to increase promotion opportunities for women and minorities in management and nonmanagement positions. ("G.E. to Pay $32 Million in Bias Pact," *New York Times,* June 16, 1978, p. D.1).

6
S. Garfinkle, "Occupations of Women and Black Workers, 1962–1974," *Monthly Labor Review,* 98 (1975): 25–36.

7
The New Haven Register, February 20, 1977.

8
Leona Toppel, *Parade Magazine,* February 20, 1977, p. 14.

9
N. Ephron, *Crazy Salad* (New York: Alfred A. Knopf, 1975), p. 55.

10
K. Gergen, "Social Psychology as History," *Journal of Personality and Social Psychology* 26 (1973): 309–320.

NOTES TO CHAPTER 2

1
M. Mead, *Male and Female* (New York: New American Library, 1955), p. 13.

2
C. Levi-Strauss, "The Family," in *Man, Culture, and Society,* ed. Harry L. Shapiro (New York: Oxford University Press, 1971), pp. 347–349.

3
T. Caplow, *The Sociology of Work* (New York: McGraw-Hill, 1954), pp. 10–11.

4
In a provocative essay about the combined effects of patriarchy and capitalism, Heidi Hartmann explains the process by which anthropologists and economists have traced historical changes in the social order and emphasized their effect on the relative location of men and women in economic institutions. H. Hartmann, "Capitalism and Patriarchy" in *Women and the Work Place*, ed. M. Blaxall and B. Reagan (Chicago: University of Chicago Press, 1976), pp. 137–170.

5
A recent representative of this approach is found in Ann Oakley's *Sex, Gender, and Society* (New York: Harper and Row, 1972), pp. 146–152.

6
Peter Filene *Him/Her/Self: Sex Roles in Modern America* (New York: Harcourt Brace Jovanovich, 1975). This work documents the historical patterns in male-female relationships in the United States.

7
Harold Wilensky, "Women's Work: Economic Growth, Ideology, Structure," *Industrial Relations* 7 (1968): 235.

8
V. Oppenheimer, "The Sex-Labeling of Jobs," *Industrial Relations* 7 (1968): 219–234.

9
R. Merton, quoted in C. Epstein, *Women's Place* (Berkeley, California: University of California Press, 1971), p. 152.

10
M. Power, "Women's Work Is Never Done—by Men: A Socioeconomic Model of Sex-Typing in Occupations," *Journal of Industrial Relations*, 17 (1975): 225–240.

11
Oppenheimer, "Sex-Labeling." p. 220.

12
R. Roderick and J. Davis, *Correlates of Atypical Job Assignment* (Columbus, Ohio: Center for Human Resource Research, Ohio State University, 1972).

13
C. Jusenius, "The Influence of Work Experience and Typicality of Occupational Assignment on Women's Earnings," *Dual Careers*, U.S. Department of Labor R&D Monograph 21 (Washington, D.C., 1976), 97–118.

14
J. C. Touhey, "Effects of Additional Women Professionals on Ratings of Occupational Prestige and Desirability," *Journal of Personality and Social Psychology* 29 (1974): 86–89.

15
Rosabeth Kanter, *Men and Women of the Corporation* (New York: Basic Books, 1977), pp. 3–11, 245–265.

16
C. Epstein, *Woman's Place* (Berkeley, Calif.: University of California Press, 1971); A. Rossi and A. Calderwood, eds., *Academic Women on the Move (New York: Russell Sage Foundation, 1973)*. There has been a recent outpouring of books on women in management. M. Fogarty et al., *Women in Top Jobs* (London: George Allen Unwin, 1971); E. Ginzberg and A. Yohalem, *Corporate Lib: Women's Challenge to Management* (Baltimore, Md.: Johns Hopkins Press, 1973); F. Gordon and M. Strober, eds., *Bringing Women into Management* (New York: McGraw-Hill, 1975); M. Hennig and A. Jardim, *The Managerial Woman* (New York: Anchor Press, Doubleday, 1977); B. Stead, *Women in Management* (Englewood Cliffs, N.J.: Prentice Hall, 1978).

A thorough compendium of research pieces about women in a range of professions, including law, medicine, teaching, academics, engineering, and architecture was edited by Athena Theodore, *The Professional Woman* (Cambridge, Mass.: Schenkman Publishing Co., 1971). This book also includes discussions about the sexual structure of professions, or occupational segregation by sex.

17
Pamela Roby made this point in a 1974 review for the Russell Sage Foundation, *The Condition of Women in Blue Collar, Industrial and Service Jobs* (Russell Sage Foundation Social Science Frontiers Series). Since that time, Terry Wetherby edited *Conversations: Working Women Talk about Doing a "Man's Job"* (Millbrae, Calif.: Les Femmes

Press, 1977), a report of interviews with women in twenty-two "male" jobs, including welder, carpenter, butcher, electrical mechanic, and law school dean.

18
Epstein, *Woman's Place,* p. 191.

19
Hennig and Jardim, *Managerial Woman.*

20
Wetherby, *Conversations.*

21
Ibid., pp. 128–129.

22
Ibid., p. 199.

23
B. Segal, "Male Nurses: A Case Study in Status Contradiction and Prestige Loss," *Social Forces* 41(1962): 31–38.

24
Ibid., pp. 32, 37, 38.

25.
A. Kadushin, "The Prestige of Social Work—Facts and Factors," *Social Work* 3(1958): 31–41.

26
H. Etzkowitz, "The Male Sister: Sexual Separation of Labor in Society," *Journal of Marriage and the Family* (1971), Vol. 33 p. 432.

27
A. M. Robinson, "Men in Nursing: Their Career Goals and Image Are Changing, *RN,* August 1973, p. 40.

28
A. Kadushin, "Men in a Woman's Profession," *Social Work* 21(1976): 440–448.

29
Ibid.

30
D. Fanshel, "Status Differentials: Men and Women in Social Work," *Social Work* 21 (1976): 448–451.

31
D. Kravetz, "Sexism in a Woman's Profession," *Social Work* 21 (1976): 421–428.

32
J. Van Maanen and E. Schein, *Toward a Theory of Organizational Socialization.* Sloan School of Management Working Paper 960-77 (Cambridge, Mass., 1977), p. 9.

33
E. C. Hughes, *Men and Their Work* (Glencoe, Ill.: The Free Press, 1958) p. 106.

34
Kanter, *Men and Women,* pp. 206–242.

35
S. Morse and K. Gergen, "Social Comparison, Self-Consistency, and the Concept of Self," *Journal of Personality and Social Psychology* 16(1970): 145–160.

36
J. Singer, "Social Comparison—Progress and Issues," *Journal of Experimental Social Psychology* 2, no. 1 (1966): 103–110.

37
L. Kidder and M. Stewart, *The Psychology of Intergroup Interactions: Conflict and Consciousness* (New York: McGraw-Hill, 1975).

38
R. Caplan et al., *Job Demands and Worker Health* (Washington, D.C.: NIOSH, 1975).

NOTES TO CHAPTER 3

1
I have been deliberately bland in my descriptions of these jobs to protect the anonymity of the organization. The epilogue discusses some of the implications of this skewed sample. It was impossible to select a nonskewed or balanced sample of "male" and "female" jobs in this company at this time.

2
The JDI, or Job Descriptive Index, was originally presented in P. C. Smith, L. M. Kendall, and C. L. Hulin, *The Measurement of Satisfaction in Work and Retirement* (Chicago: Rand McNally, 1969). The JDI instrument is generally considered to be a reliable and valid measure of five dimensions of job satisfaction. Permission for use of the JDI, which is copyrighted material, was obtained from Bowling Green State University.

3
The Procedure: To understand and interpret the results of this type of regression analysis, it is important to describe aspects of the dummy coding operation before describing the analysis itself. Three approaches to coding were used. Quantitative variables (length of time in job) were assigned their original values. Qualitative variables were coded 1 or 0 depending on whether the category characteristic was present. For example, for match of

employee, if the sex of employee and supervisor matched, the value of 0 was assigned; if the sex of the two did not match, a value of 1 was assigned to that person for that variable. The third approach to coding involved the nominal variable, job name. For manageability, the three small clerical jobs were merged into one category. Then all jobs were recoded on a dummy coding basis (person assigned a 1 if in job and a 0 otherwise). Because of matrix operations, occupants of job 8 were not categorized, nor assigned a value of 0,1. By this procedure we established a comparative situation between job type 8 and all the other jobs, facilitating analysis of the comparative effects of the different jobs on worker satisfaction. Finally variables representing the noted interactions were computed, based on the values of their components, by simply multiplying the values of the relevant variables.

The first step in the analysis itself was cross validation. For cross validation, the analysis was done separately on comparable halves of the original sample of 100. Confidence in the results is high because essentially the same results were obtained in both subsamples ($n=50$). For this reason, this discussion reports values obtained in the large sample analysis.

For parsimony the backward elimination approach was used, based on appropriate coding of interactions and dummy variables. Then to reach the final equation from the full model, regression analysis was run on the full model and the variable with the lowest F value was dropped from the equation. That equation was then subjected to regression analysis, and the variable with the smallest F value was dropped for the next analysis. Following each step of the analysis, both R^2 (the amount of sample variation in the independent variable explained by a set of explanatory variables) and $\bar{R}^2$ (the amount of sample variation explained, modified by the degrees of freedom, and thus affected by the number of variables in the equation) were examined to ensure the continuing quality of the reduced model. The final model was selected when the F values for all variables left in the equation were significant.

4
John Bassler introduced me to this valuable tool, from R. Darlington, "Multiple Regression in Psychological Research and Practice," *Psychological Bulletin* 69(1968): 161–182.

5
E. Locke, "The Nature and Causes of Job Satisfaction," in *Handbook of Industrial and Organizational Psychology,* ed. M. Dunnette (Chicago: Rand McNally, 1976), pp. 1297–1351.

6
Ibid., p. 1319.

7
Ibid., p. 1320.

8
Ibid.

9
J. McGrath, "Stress and Behavior in Organizations" in Dunnette, *Handbook,* pp. 1351–1396.

10
Locke, "Job Satisfaction," p. 1320.

11
H. Selye, *The Stress of Life* (New York: McGraw-Hill, 1956), p. 124.

12
Ibid.

NOTES TO CHAPTER 4

1
The spotlight here is on the work experiences of the sex-atypical employees, through their reports and the reports of others in settings that New Types had entered. Since most of the Same Type employees included in this study had been part of a work situation into which a New Type had been introduced, I use both sets of reports as part of a composite picture, with no implication about *shared* experience in any one situation. Similarly, because all these reports are based on the memories of the interviewees and not on direct observation by the researcher, these depictions rely wholly on the fallibility of human observation and memory.

2
It is hard to know whether this was due to actual differences in feeling, actual differences in acknowledgment of feeling, actual differences in expression of acknowledgment of feeling, actual openness or nondefensiveness with the interviewer, and so on. The fact remains that there was a difference between men and women in their reference to and appreciation of prejob question and apprehension.

3
H. Meyer and M. Lee, "The Integration of Females into Male-Oriented Jobs: Experiences of Certain Public Utility Companies," University of South Florida, 1976.

4
It may be that the wording of the question was charged

enough to generate more tepid responses than we might have had with an open-ended and descriptive question. Use of the word *rejecting* may have elicited counterreaction from participants. Other questions about early inclusion that did not mention the word *rejection* seemed to have elicited more descriptive responses from participants.

5
E. C. Hughes, *Men and Their Work* (Glencoe, Ill.: The Free Press, 1958), pp. 108–109.

6
Ibid.

7
Ibid.

8
C. Alderfer, "Group and Intergroup Relations," in *Improving Life at Work,* ed. J. R. Hackman and J. L. Suttle (Santa Monica, Calif.: Goodyear Publishing Co., 1977), pp. 227–296.

9
Ibid.

10
E. Miller and A. K. Rice, *Systems of Organization* (London: Tavistock Publications, 1967).

11
Rosabeth Kanter, *Men and Women of the Corporation* (New York: Basic Books, 1977), p. 230.

12
Ibid.

13
C. Alderfer, personal communication, June 1977.

NOTES TO CHAPTER 5

1
M. Fasteau, *The Male Machine* (New York: Dell Publishing Co., 1975).

2
R. Levine and D. Campbell, *Ethnocentrism: Theories of Conflict, Ethnic Attitudes, and Group Behavior* (New York: J. Wiley and Sons, 1972), p. 194.

3
Ibid., p. 196.

4
Ibid.

5
A. Kadushin, "Men in a Woman's Profession," *Social Work* 21 (1976): 466.

227
Notes to
pp. 122–132

NOTES TO CHAPTER 6

1
David Cohen argues for an appreciation of the theoretical and empirical uncertainty behind the social experiment. Cohen persuasively contrasts the origins and outcome possibilities of social experiments compared to more controlled research situations. He spells out the difficult but necessary limitations on social policy and program research ["The Value of Social Experiments," in *Planned Variation in Education,* edited by A. Rivlan and R. Timpane (Washington, D.C.: Brookings Institution, 1975), p. 53].

2
Keneth Gergen has developed this idea in the form of the "crystallization of inequity"—a concept that explains why people maintain beliefs about themselves and others even when those beliefs sustain an inequitable or disadvantaged position for an individual. As Gergen notes, "The development and solidification of norms may seal the fate for the low-power person for long periods of time. As the norms become sanctified and ritualized, inequity on an objective level comes to be viewed as equitable" [*The Psychology of Behavior Exchange* (Reading, Mass.: Addison-Wesley, 1969), p. 90].

3
Examples of this orientation include Rosabeth Kanter, *Men and Women of the Corporation* (New York: Basic Books, 1977); M. Lockheed and K. Hall, "Conceptualizing Sex as a Status Characteristic: Applications to Leadership Training Strategies," *Journal of Social Issues,* 32 (1976): 111–124; G. Zellman, "The Role of Structural Factors in Limiting Women's Institutional Participation," *Journal of Social Issues* 32 (1976): 33–47.

4
R. Levine and D. Campbell, *Ethnocentrism: Theories of Conflict, Ethnic Activities, and Group Behavior* (New York: J. Wiley and Sons, 1972).

5
An interesting example of the "negative discrepancy" and "status inconsistency" is suggested by the recent selection of female astronauts for the first time; six women were included among the thirty-five persons selected for training in 1978. Of the six women selected, two had M.D. degrees and four had Ph.D.'s. Although I am unsure of the academic credentials of the 1978

crop of male astronauts, previous groups that I know of did not have the range of academic degrees represented in the sample of women. Here, too, in a relatively new occupation, women seem to have had to make up for their deficiencies in a male sex-typed field with extra credentials.

6
S. Taylor and S. Fiske, "The Token in a Small Group: Research Findings and Theoretical Implications," in *Psychology and Politics: Collected Papers,* ed. J. Sweeney (New Haven, Conn.: Yale University Press, 1976).

7
New York Times, April 24, 1977, p. 1.

8
J. Rosenbaum, "A Focused Group Study of Men in Management," 1976; C. Schreiber, "A Focused Group Study of Women in Management," Yale University, 1976.

9
See Edgar Schein's thorough discussion of the possible design and function of such a mechanism in "Increasing Organizational Effectiveness through Better Human Resource Planning and Development," *Sloan Management Review* 19 (1977): 1–21.

10
Ernest Green, Prefatory Remarks in U.S. Department of Labor, *Dictionary of Occupational Titles,* 4th rev. ed.

NOTES TO THE EPILOGUE

1
E. Cronbach, "Beyond the Two Disciplines of Scientific Psychology," *American Psychologist,* Vol. 30, #2, February 1975, p. 124.

2
J. Douglass, "Investigative Social Research: Individual and Team Field Research." Department of Sociology, University of California, San Diego, 1974.

3
E. Goffman, *The Presentation of Self in Everyday Life* (Garden City, N.Y.: Doubleday and Co., 1959), p. 15.

4
Ibid., p. 144.

5
Cronbach, "Beyond Scientific Pscyhology," p. 125.

6
Ibid., p. 126.

7
R. Guion, "Synthetic Validity in a Small Company: A Demonstration," *Personnel Psychology* 18(1965): 49–63.

8
C. Alderfer, "Comparison of Questionnaire Responses with and without Preceding Interview," *Journal of Applied Psychology* 52(1968): 335–340.

9
H. Wilensky, "Measures and Effect of Social Mobility," in *Social Structure and Mobility in Economic Development,* ed. N. Smelser and S. M. Lipset, Boston, Mass. (Routledge and Kegan Paul, 1966), pp 94–140.

10
Caplan, et al. *Job Demands.*

11
P. Smith, L. Kendall, and C. Hulin, *The Measurement of Satisfaction in Work and Retirement* (Chicago: Rand McNally, 1969).

12
J. R. Hackman, *You and Your Job: JDS Short Form* (New Haven: Department of Administrative Sciences, Yale University, Mimeo 1976).

BIBLIOGRAPHY

Acker, J., and Van Houten, D. "Differential Recruitment and Control: The Sex Structuring of Organizations." *Administrative Science Quarterly* 19 (1974): 152–63.

Alderfer, C. "Group and Intergroup Relations." in *Improving Life at Work,* edited by J. R. Hackman and J. L. Suttle. Santa Monica, Calif.: Goodyear Publishing Co., 1977, pp. 227–296.

————. "Comparison of Questionnaire Responses with and without Preceding Interviews." *Journal of Applied Psychology* 52 (1968): 335–340.

Alderfer, C., and Brown, D. "Designing an Empathic Questionnaire for Organizational Research." *Journal of Applied Psychology* 56 (1972): 456–460.

Almquist, E. "Women in the Labor Force." *Signs* 2, no. 4 (1977): 843–856.

Angrist, S. "Social Science: An Overview." *Signs* 1, no. 1 (1975): 175–183.

————. "The Study of Sex Roles." *Journal of Social Issues* 25, 215–232.

Barker, R. Q., and Wright, H. F. *Midwest and Its Children.* New York: Harper and Row, 1955.

Bird, C. *Everything A Woman Needs to Know to Get Paid What She's Worth.* New York: Bantam Books, 1974.

Boals, K. "Political Science," *Signs,* 1, no. 1 (1975): 161–174.

Campbell, D. T. "Stereotypes and the Perception of Group Differences." *American Psychologist* 22 (1967): 812–829.

Caplan, R., Cobb, S., French, J., Harrison, R., and Pinneau, S. *Job Demands and Worker Health.* Washington, D.C.: National Institute of Occupational Health and Safety, 1975.

Caplow, T. *The Sociology of Work.* New York: McGraw-Hill, 1954.

Chapman, J. "Economics." *Signs* 1, no. 1 (1975): 139–147.

Cooper, C., and Payne, R., eds. *Stress at Work.* New York: John Wiley and Sons, 1978.

Cottle, T. J., and Klineberg, S. L. *The Present of Things Future.* New York: The Free Press, 1974.

Cronbach, E. "Beyond the Two Disciplines of Scientific Psychology." *American Psychologist,* 30, (1975): pp. 116–127.

Daniels, A. K. *A Survey of Research Concerns on Women's Issues.* Washington, D.C.: Association of American Colleges, Mimeo 1975.

Darlington, R. "Multiple Regression in Psychological Research and Practice." *Psychological Bulletin* 69 (1968): 161–182.

Douglass, J. "Investigative Social Research: Individual and Team Field Research." 1974.

Ephron, N. *Crazy Salad.* New York: Alfred A. Knopf, 1975.

232

Epstein, C. *Woman's Place.* Berkeley, Calif.: University of California Press, 1970.

Etzioni, A., ed. *The Semi-Professions and Their Organization.* New York: The Free Press, 1969.

Etzkowitz, H. "The Male Sister: Sexual Separation of Labor in Society." *Journal of Marriage and the Family.* Vol. 33 (August 1971): 431–434.

Fanshel, David. "Status Differentials: Men and Women in Social Work." *Social Work* 21 (1976): 448–451.

Fasteau, M. *The Male Machine.* New York: Dell Publishing Co., 1975.

Filene, P. *Him/Her/Self: Sex Roles in Modern America.* New York: Harcourt Brace Jovanovich, 1975.

Fogarty, M., Allen, A., Allen, I., and Walters, P. *Women in Top Jobs.* London: George Allen Unwin, 1971.

French, J. "Person-Role Fit." in *Occupational Stress,* edited by A. McLean. Springfield, Ill.: Charles C. Thomas, 1974, pp. 70–80.

Garfinkle, S. "Occupations of Women and Black Workers, 1962–1974." *Monthly Labor Review* 98 (1975): 25–36.

Garson, B. *All the Livelong Day.* New York: Penguin Books, 1977.

Gates, M. "Occupational Segregation and the Law." In *Women and the Workplace,* edited by M.

Blaxall and B. Reagan. Chicago: University of Chicago Press, 1976, pp. 61–74.

"G. E. to Pay $32 Million in Bias Pact." *New York Times,* June 16, 1978, pp. D1–D4.

Gergen, K. "Social Psychology as History." *Journal of Personality and Social Psychology* 26 (1973): 309–320.

————. *The Psychology of Behavior Exchange.* Reading, Mass.: Addison-Wesley Publishing Co., 1969.

Gibbard, G. "Individuation, Fusion, and Role Specialization." In *Analysis of Groups,* edited by G. Gibbard, J. Hartman, and R. Mann. New York: Jossey-Bass, 1974, pp. 247–266.

Ginzberg, E. and Yohalem, A. *Corporate Lib: Women's Challenge to Management.* Baltimore Md.: Johns Hopkins Press, 1973.

Goffman, E. *Stigma: Notes on the Management of Spoiled Identity.* Englewood Cliffs, N.J.: Prentice-Hall, 1963.

————. *The Presentation of Self in Everyday Life.* Garden City, N.Y.: Doubleday and Co., 1959.

Gordon, C. "Development of Evaluated Role Identities." *Annual Review of Sociology* 2 (1976): 405–433.

Gordon, F., and Strober, M., eds. *Bringing Women into Management.* New York: McGraw-Hill, 1975.

Gross, E. "Plus Ca Change: Sexual Structure of Occupations over Time." *Social Problems* 1 (1968): 225–258.

Guion, R. "Synthetic Validity in a Small Company: A Demonstration." *Personnel Psychology* 18 (1965): 49–63.

Hackman, J. R. *You and Your Job: JDS Short Form.* Department of Administrative Sciences, Yale University, Mimeo, 1976.

Hackman, J. R., and Oldham, G. *The Job Diagnostic Survey: An Instrument for the Diagnosis of Jobs and the Evaluation of Job Redesign Projects.* Technical Report No. 4. Department of Administrative Sciences, Yale University, 1974.

Howe, L. K. *Pink-Collar Workers.* New York: Avon Books, 1977.

Huber, J. "Sociology." *Signs* 1, no. 3 (1976): 685–698.

Hughes, E. C. *Men and Their Work.* Glencoe, Ill.: The Free Press, 1958.

Jusenius, Carol. "The Influence of Work Experience and Typicality of Occupational Assignment on Women's Earnings." In *Dual Careers,* U.S. Department of Labor, R & D Monograph 21. Washington, D.C., 1976, pp. 97–118.

Kadushin, A. "Men in a Woman's Profession." *Social Work* 21 (1976): 440–447.

———. "The Prestige of Social Work: Facts and Factors." *Social Work* 3 (1958): 31–41.

Kanter, R. *Men and Women of the Corporation.* New York: Basic Books, 1977.

Kanter, R. "Women and the Structure of Organizations." In *Another Voice,* edited by R. Kanter and M. Millman. New York: Doubleday, 1975, pp. 34–75.

Kerlinger, F. *Foundations of Behavioral Research.* 2nd ed., New York: Holt, Rhinehart and Winston, 1973.

Kerlinger, F. M., and Pedhazur, E. J. *Multiple Regression in Behavioral Research.* New York: Holt, Rhinehart and Winston, 1973.

Kidder, L., and Stewart, M. *The Psychology of Intergroup Relations: Conflict and Consciousness.* New York: McGraw-Hill, 1975.

Kohen, A. *"Women and the Economy."* College of Administrative Science, Ohio State University, 1975.

Kravetz, D. "Sexism in a Woman's Profession." *Social Work* 21 (1976): 421–428.

"Lagging Behind: Though More Women Work, Job Equality Fails to Materialize." *Wall Street Journal,* July 6, 1976, pp. 1, 13.

Laws, J. "The Psychology of Tokenism: An Analysis." *Sex Roles* 1 (1975): 51–67.

Levine, R., and Campbell, D. *Ethnocentrism: Theories of Conflict, Ethnic Attitudes, and Group Behavior.* New York: J. Wiley and Sons, 1972.

Levinson, D. L. "Role, Personality, and Social Structure in the Organizational Setting." *Journal of Abnormal and Social Psychology* 58 (1959): 170–180.

LeMasters, E. E. *Blue-Collar Aristocrats: Life-Styles at a Working-Class Tavern,* Madison, Wisc.: University of Wisconsin Press, 1975.

Lipman-Blumen, J., and Tickamyer, A. "Sex Roles in Transition." *Annual Review of Sociology* 1 (1975): 297–337.

Locke, E. "The Nature and Causes of Job Satisfaction." In *Handbook of Industrial and Organizational Psychology,* edited by M. Dunnette. Chicago: Rand McNally, 1976, pp. 1297–1351.

Lockheed, M., and Hall, K. "Conceptualizing Sex as a Status Characteristic: Applications to Leadership Training Strategies." *Journal of Social Issues* 32 (1976): 111–124.

Loring, R., and Wells, T. *Breakthrough: Women into Management.* New York: Van Nostrand Rheinhold, 1972.

Mead, M. *Male and Female.* New York: New American Library, 1955.

Mednick, M. "The New Psychology of Women: A Feminist Analysis." In *Perspectives on the Psychology of Women,* edited by J. E. Gullahorn and E. Donalson. Washington, D.C.: Winston and Sons, forthcoming.

Meyer, H., and Lee, M. "The Integration of Females into Male-Oriented Jobs: Experiences of Certain Public Utility Companies." University of South Florida, 1976.

Miller, E. J., and Rice, A. K. *Systems of Organization.* London: Tavistock Publications, 1967.

McGrath, J. "Stress and Behavior in Organizations." In *Handbook of Industrial and Organizational Psychology,* edited by M. Dunnette. Chicago: Rand McNally, 1976, pp. 1351–1396.

Morse, S., and Gergen, K. "Social Comparison, Self-Consistency, and the Concept of Self." *Journal of Personality and Social Psychology* 16 (1970): 145–160.

National Manpower Council. *Womanpower.* New York: Columbia University Press, 1957.

Neter, J., and Wasserman, W. *Applied Linear Statistical Models.* Homewood, Ill.: Richard D. Irwin, 1974.

Nie, N. H., Hull, C. H., Jenkins, J. A., Steinbrenner, K., and Bent, D. H. *Statistical Package for the Social Sciences.* 2nd ed. New York: McGraw-Hill, 1975.

Oakley, Ann. *Sex, Gender, and Society.* New York: Harper and Row, 1972.

Oppenheimer, V. "Demographic Influence on Female Employment and the Status of Women." *American Journal of Sociology* (1973): 946–961.

Oppenheimer, V. The Sex-Labelling of Jobs. *Industrial Relations* 7 (1968): 219–234.

Parlee, M. "Psychology." *Signs* 1, no. 1 (1975): 119–138.

Pleck. J. "Masculinity–Femininity: Current and Alternative Paradigms." *Sex Roles* 1, no. 2 (1975): 161–178.

Power, M. "Woman's Work is Never Done—by Men: A Socioeconomic Model of Sex-Typing in Occupations." *Journal of Industrial Relations* 17 (1975): 225–240.

Pressman, J., and Wildavsky, A. *Implementation.* Berkeley, Calif.: University of California Press, 1973.

Ritzer, G. *Man and His Work: Conflict and Change.* New York: Appleton-Century-Crofts, 1972.

Rivlin, A., and Timpane, M. *Planned Variation in Education: Should We Give Up or Try Harder.* Washington, D.C.: Brookings Institution, 1975.

Rizzo, J., House, R., and Lirtzman, S. "Role Conflict and Ambiguity in Complex Organizations." *Administrative Science Quarterly* 15 (1970): 150–163.

Robinson, A. M. "Men in Nursing: Their Career Goals and Image Are Changing." *RN* 36 (August 1973): 36–41.

Roby, P. *The Conditions of Women in Blue-Collar, Industrial, and Service Jobs.* Russell Sage Foundation Social Science Frontiers Series, Mimeo, 1974.

Roderick, R., and J. Davis. Correlates of Atypical Job Assignment. Columbus, Ohio: Center for Human Resources Research, Ohio State University, Technical Report, 1972.

Rosenbaum, J. "A Focused Group Study of Men in Management." Unpublished paper, Yale University, 1976.

Rosenberg, B. G., and Sutton-Smith, B. *Sex and Identity.* New York: Holt, Rhinehart and Winston, 1972.

Rosenthal, R. *Experimental Effects in Behavioral Research.* New York: Appleton-Century-Crofts, 1966.

Rossi, A., and Calderwood, A., eds. *Academic Women on the Move.* New York: Russell Sage Foundation, 1973.

Sarason, S. "Jewishness, Blackness and the Nature-Nurture Controversy." *American Psychologist* 28 (1973): 962–971.

Schein, E. "Increasing Organizational Effectiveness through Better Human Resource Planning and Development." *Sloan Management Review* 19 (1977): 1–21.

Schreiber, C. "Occupational Choice and Women's Work." Technical Report, School of Organization and Management, Yale University, 1975.

236

Schreiber, C. "A Focused Group Study of Women in Management." Technical Report, School of Organization and Management, Yale University, 1976.

Seligman, M. *Helplessness.* San Francisco, California.: W. H. Freeman and Co., 1975.

Seltiz, C., and Cook, S. W. "Can Research in Social Science Be Both Socially Useful and Scientifically Meaningful?" *American Sociological Review* 13 (1948): 454–459.

Selye, Hans. *The Stress of Life.* New York: McGraw-Hill, 1956.

Singer, J. Social Comparison: Progress and Issues. *Journal of Experimental Social Psychology* 2 (1966): 103–110.

Smith, P. C., Kendall, L. M., and Hulen, C. L. *The Measurement of Satisfaction in Work and Retirement.* Chicago: Rand McNally, 1969.

Smith, T. "Sociocultural Incongruity and Change: A Review of Empirical Findings. In *Social Stress and Cardiovascular Disease,* edited by S. L. Syme and L. G. Reeder. *Millbank Memorial Fund Quarterly* 45, 1967. (April): Part 2, pp. 17–46.

Stack, C. et al. "Anthropology." *Signs* 1, no. 1 (1975): 147–159.

Stead, B. *Women in Management.* Englewood Cliffs, N.J.: Prentice-Hall, 1978.

Stoller, R., *Sex and Gender.* New York: Science House, 1968.

Taylor, S., and Fiske, S. "The Token in a Small Group: Research Findings and Theoretical Implications." In *Psychology and Politics: Collected Papers,* edited by J. Sweeney. New Haven, Conn.: Yale University Press, 1976.

Theodore, A. *The Professional Woman.* Cambridge, Mass.: Schenkmans Publishing Co., 1971.

Theorell, T., and Rahe, R. H. *Life Changes in Relation to the Onset of Myocardial Infarction: A Pilot Study.* Stockholm, Sweden: Karolinska Institutet, 1970.

Toppel, L. "Anecdote." *Parade Magazine,* February 20, 1977, p. 14.

Toren, N. *Social Work: The Case of a Semiprofession.* Beverly Hills, Calif., Sage Press, 1972.

Touhey, J. "Effects of Additional Women Professionals on Ratings of Occupational Prestige and Desirability." *Journal of Personality and Social Psychology* 29 (1974): 86–89.

Turner, R. H. Role Taking, Role Standpoint, and Reference Group Behavior. *American Journal of Sociology* 61 (1955–1956): 316–328.

U.S. Department of Labor, *U.S. Working Women: A Chartbook.* Bulletin 1880, Bureau of Labor Statistics, Washington, D.C., 1975.

U.S. Department of Labor, *U.S. Working Women: A Databook.* Bulletin 1977, Bureau of Labor Statistics, Washington, D.C., 1977.

Van Maanen, J., ed. *Organizational Careers.* New York: John Wiley and Sons, 1977.

Van Maanen, J., and Schein, E. "Toward a Theory of Organizational Socialization." Sloan School of Management Working Paper, nos. 960-77. Cambridge, Mass., 1977.

VanSell, M., Brief, A., and Schuler, R. *Role Conflict and Role Ambiguity: A Review and Synthesis of the Literature,* Iowa City, Iowa: College of Business Administration, University of Iowa, 1976.

Wallace, P., ed. *Equal Employment Opportunity and the AT&T Case.* Cambridge, Mass.: MIT Press, 1976.

Walster, E., and Walster, R. "Effect of Expecting To Be Liked on Choice of Associates." *Journal of Abnormal Psychology,* 67 (1963): 402–404.

Wiggin, Jerry. *Personality and Prediction: Principles of Personality Assessment.* Reading, Mass.: Addison-Wesley Publishing Co., 1973.

Wilensky, H. "Measures and Effect of Social Mobility." In *Social Structure and Mobility in Economic Development,* edited by N. J. Smelser and S. M. Lipset. Routledge and Kegan Paul, 1966, pp. 94–140.

————. "Women's Work: Economic Growth, Ideology, Structure." *Industrial Relations* 7 (1968): 235–248.

Zellman, G. "The Role of Structural Factors in Limiting Women's Institutional Participation." *Journal of Social Issues* 32 (1976): 33–47.

INDEX